Once Upo
Wartime

by Molly Burkett & Robert Street

Molly Burkett (signature)

Words © Molly Burkett & Robert Street

ISBN N° 1 903172 14 4

No part of this publication may be reproduced or transmitted in any way or by any means, including electronic storage and retrieval, without prior permission of the publisher.

Produced by **TUCANN**design&print, 19 High Street, Heighington, Lincoln LN4 1RG
Telephone & Fax: 01522 790009
www.tucann.co.uk

STRANGER IN A STRANGE LAND
INTELLEGENCE CORPS - Ron Pang

I never knew my grandparents. My mother's father was a policeman and he had been killed by the suffragettes. My father was Chinese. His parents had sent him and his sister to be educated in Hong Kong. There were three problems in China, famine, flood and disease. His family perished in one of the plagues and my father and his sister never went back to their village. My father joined a seamen's tong, a kind of brotherhood They helped him get his British Seaman's Book (Board of Trade papers) and he signed on a British ship as a fireman and trimmer. After the First World War, he came down to London and worked at the Trocadero which was where he met my mother.

My father sent my sister and me to a Chinese school in Gower Street to learn Chinese. There are several dialects, Mandarin, Canton and so on. I managed to master the language but I was never much good at writing it down. But I was good at English and when I left school I got a job as an office boy. Then I went into service. It was a good job. I had my own room and clean sheets on the bed and three good meals a day. I was paid ten shillings a week all found. When the war broke out, his Lordship shut the house up and I was out of a job. I went to an agency and got a job as a footman with Lady Hood at Lower Brook Street. But I felt unsettled. I was seventeen and Dunkirk had been evacuated. I felt I should be helping so I went to the headquarters of the Territorials at Dukes Road to sign up. A sergeant was sitting behind the desk with his head in a newspaper. I stood and waited. Then he said, "Yes." I told him I had come to join the army and he told me to return the next afternoon at two o'clock. There were three of us that reported the next afternoon. The sergeant still had his head in what looked like the same newspaper. He lowered it to ask me how old I was and he gave me a form to fill in. I put down footman as my occupation and he didn't know what it was. He thought it was something to do with horses. I volunteered to serve for the duration of the war. I was sworn in and given the King's shilling. I've still got it. I was given my attestation papers and a travel warrant for Folkestone. I had been asked which Regiment I wanted. I chose the West Kents, the Buffs, because I liked the dragon on their badge. When I first went home in my uniform, my father was very excited when he saw the dragon badge. He kept repeating, "Lucky, lucky, lucky." The dragon is a good luck symbol in China.

When I got off the train at Folkestone, Sandgate, there was one other fellow standing at the end of the platform. He couldn't have been more than five feet tall. He came up and asked if I was joining up as well so we agreed to go together. The station master rang the Drill hall and they sent a 15 hundredweight lorry to pick us up and take us back to the hall where we were each handed an enamel mug full of hot, sweet tea. Then we piled back into the truck and were taken to what in peace time had been a girls' school. That was where I met my new colleagues.

All our N.C.O.s had escaped from Dunkirk. They had had a rough time out there and of the two battalions that had been in France, not enough had returned to make up a single one. We were the 6th H.D. Battalion. I didn't know what H.D. meant but I soon found out. It stood for Home Defence. We were all lads not considered old enough to serve abroad. The old lags called us the baby Buffs.

The N.C.O.s set about making us into soldiers but the Greek fellow I had met on the station was a pain. He couldn't march. I think it was probably because his legs were so short. He could not get one foot in front of the other in the right order. We were often called back for extra marching practice because he was always out of step. He wasn't any better with a rifle. It seemed bigger than him anyway. He always seemed to be getting it stuck in the most awkward positions. He was put on so many charges that we all began to feel sorry for him. He was always peeling potatoes or getting up early to make the porage for extra duties. He almost lived in the kitchen. He made so much porridge that he began to show a real aptitude for it and he was transferred to the Catering Corps. He was the first one of us to be posted. He became a company cook.

We spent a lot of time on guard duty. It was a tense time in England. The British were expecting the Germans to invade at any time and we were on the look out for German parachutists. We stood to every morning and evening, two hours at dawn and two at dusk because that was the time they thought the Germans would come.

I saw my first dead body when I was on guard duty at Shakespeare Cliff Halt, between Dover and Folkestone. I saw what I thought was a piece of tarpaulin being tossed about in the waves. It was my mate, Danny Keen, who recognised it as a body. We made our way down to the water's edge. He was face down in the water and my first thought was that I had to turn him over so that he wouldn't drown. I took hold of his helmet and turned it over and it came away in my hands along with his hair and ears. There was no face. We sent back to ask what to do and were told to pull the body above the water line and wait until someone came. The corporal wasn't long in coming and he identified it immediately as the body of a German pilot. We found out later that his name was Petigruber. I had noticed an automatic, a Walther, in his belt so I slipped it under my battledress. I thought it would make a nice souvenir but Bob Cork, the lance corporal, had seen it too and I had to hand it over to him.

Danny Keen and I were good pals. We had joined up on the same day. He was Jewish. We called him Danny but his real name was Danziel. Later on, he joined the paras the same as I did. He landed at Arnhem and that was the last anyone saw of him. Nobody knows what happened to him. He didn't have to go. The Rabbi had called all the Jews to a meeting and told them what could happen to them if they were captured by the Germans. He told them that none of them needed to go but they all refused to consider dropping out. The other paras had been waiting outside and they cheered when they came out.

We saw a lot of Kent during those first few months. We were posted to Canterbury first, then we went to Hawkinge and then on to Whitstable. I fired my first gun in anger at Hawkinge. We were on duty at the airfield and it was strafed by a German 109. I had a Lewis gun and I shot at it but it did more for my morale than for the war effort. The fighter flew so fast, it must have been over the horizon before my first shots were airborne.

Then I went AWOL - absent without leave. There had been heavy bombing raids on London and I hadn't had the usual weekly letter from my mother. I was worried about them. A lad from the East end of London was in the same state so we agreed to go together. We knew we would have to be back within seventy two hours. If we stayed away any longer than that, we would have been deserters and that was a court martial offence. We hitched lifts and we reached Waterloo Station when there was a raid on. An announcement came over the tannoy telling everyone to wear their tin helmets. We needed them. We went out into the street despite a Redcap trying to stop us and we were bombarded with shrapnel from our own guns. The scene that met our eyes was indescribable, the blitz at its worse but I made my way through it all. I had to know my family were alright. When I did get there, my father was in the kitchen eating a jam sandwich and he didn't seem to have a care in the world. My mother was sheltering in the underground station with the two boys. They had been evacuated but they kept coming home.

I waited until my mother came home in the morning and we had a breakfast of sorts. Rationing was in force and there was no spare food. An extra mouth to feed could be a problem. Then I went out to look at the damage. A block of flats along the road had been flattened and men were trying to clear it. A warden shouted out to me, "Come and give us a hand soldier." I scrambled over the rubble and set to. Another warden called out for help. He had found a leg. I went to help him and we feverishly pulled bricks and wood away. There was a dusty smell and everything was wet because the water mains had broken but fortunately, there were no cellars to these flats. Cellars could be a real problem with bomb damage because water could collect in them and people sheltering there could be drowned. We managed to clear the leg and part of a nightdress was revealed and that was all there was. There was no sign of the rest of the body. They found it all in the end and it was carried away in pieces in a grey blanket. This got to me more than finding the pilot's body the previous month. He was part of the war. This lady wasn't.

I met my friend the next day as we had arranged and we made our way back to the barracks. We had to reach them on our own so that we could be dealt with by our own people. We made it alright. We were put on extra duties and lost three days' pay, that was six days pay in all because we weren't paid for the three days we'd been AWOL, but it was worth it to know that my family were O.K.

The training was hard and we were hard. We learned how to look after ourselves. The Canadians were a tough lot but they didn't pick an argument with the Buffs, nor did the Poles. I suppose that was why I reacted the way I did when the corporal came for me. We had been on Church parade and had returned to our huts. I started making my bed, as did some of the others. We should have done that after dinner but we started on ours straight away. Making a bed up in the army doesn't mean getting it ready for sleep. The blankets had to be folded and our kit laid out in a certain order. Everything had to be cleaned or polished until it shone. Then the corporal came in and he shouted that our beds should not have been made down. He came down the hut and from the minute he had come into the hut, his eyes had been fixed on me. On the way, he picked up a steel helmet. Those helmets could be used as weapons and I knew it. Men scraped them on wet concrete until the brims were sharp. They could be lethal in a fight. As he came nearer, he called me a yellow bastard. I was being forced into a corner. I picked up a knife and threatened him. That was a court martial offence and he charged me. I was taken to the guard house and locked up. The next day I was taken under escort with my hands handcuffed to Ashford, the Army Battalion HQ, and put in a cell there. The next morning, a captain came to see me. He was to be my defending officer. He was Jewish and he was good. He had been a solicitor in civilian life. He already had a copy of the statement I had made and he had seen witnesses who had confirmed my story. He had also checked out the corporal and discovered that he had not only missed Church parade, he had spent the time drinking in the mess. He also had a statement from a sergeant who claimed that the corporal had been drunk the night before.

I was upset when I was marched in for the Court Martial. The whole thing was intimidating for a seventeen year old but the defending officer spoke up for me and I was acquitted. I had a real welcome when I got back to the barracks and I don't think I bought a drink for three weeks. The corporal was charged and demoted to a private. He immediately requested that he be moved and we never heard of him again.

We had two weeks embarkation leave and then set sail on a troopship from Avonmouth. We had no idea where we were going but we soon settled down for the night in hammocks.

When we got up in the morning, we discovered that we were in the middle of a huge convoy of ships. Destroyers were circling us the whole time and aeroplanes flying overhead. We lost the air escort as we went further into the

Atlantic. There was a tension on board and boredom too. We had P.E. each morning which was running round the deck in our P.E. kit and our army boots. We had boat drill every day but it wasn't long before we had read all the books and told all the jokes we knew. We spent most of the time playing housey, housey or cards or betting. I became a fanatic at cards, poker and blackjack mostly and, as for betting, well we'd bet on anything.

Then we went on deck one morning and found we were on our own. The rest of the convoy had disappeared. We were issued with tropical kit, drill trousers and shirts, Bombay bowlers (pith helmets) and puttees. Those puttees were invaluable in the desert. They stopped the sand getting into your boots and between your toes. The sand was clean enough but it would rub you raw and cause problems. The ship zigzagged its way onwards, then one of the sailors told me that we would be seeing land shortly. I asked him how he knew and he told me to look at the colour of the sea. There was a yellow hue to it.

"That's the silt being washed out from a river," he said.

It wasn't long before sea gulls were following in our wake and we saw the coast. We anchored outside the harbour and discovered that we were at the port of Bahia in Brazil. We took on stores as well, coal being one of the most important. We were ordered to keep all the port holes closed while they were loading it, it was so dusty. We hadn't seen bananas since the war had started and now we watched as a crane swung a huge net full on board. Only the ship's officers and our own senior officers were allowed on shore. We had to stay on board and watch what was going on. It looked really tempting. We could see the young boys swimming in the harbour.

"Shall we leg it?" my friend suggested.

We could easily have swum to the shore but one of the sailors stopped us. He said the sea was too dangerous. We thought he meant there were sharks about but he explained that it was the jellyfish that were dangerous. They were huge and their sting could have killed us. They were Portuguese Man o' War with tentacles ten feet long that could paralyse their prey. They came in on an oncoming tide. That was why no-one swam until the tide turned.

We were issued with bottles of soda water mixed with quinine each day. Quinine was the only known way to combat malaria. There was no beer on board. All troopships were dry, so we drank the mixture and used our imaginations.

Then there was more land ahead and we were on deck watching it come nearer. We went through hundreds and hundreds of orange boxes intermingled with life jackets and rafts floating on the surface. One of the sailors told us that a ship must have gone down. We wondered what would have happened to the crew but the sailor simply shrugged his shoulders and said that it was shark waters.

In the early morning I saw Table Mountain with its tablecloth of clouds. I knew where we were immediately. We had been having lectures each day and one of the officers had talked about South Africa and shown us slides of Table Mountain. We had also had a lecture on sexually transmitted diseases illustrated with colour slides. That had scared us to death. We would have had to be drunk if any of us had gone with a native woman after that.

We landed at Durban and that was where we did a runner. It was such a relief to leave the ship. We had been on it for five weeks. We had day passes and had to be back on board ship by 23.59 hours. We knew we would be put on a charge if we were late but we had reached the stage where we didn't care. We weren't drunk but were in a stupid state. We had been warned about going down the Old Dutch Road where the hatwe gangs hung out but the rest of the world was ours. My pal said why didn't he knock a car off and we could travel. I told him there was no need to knock anything off, we had enough money with five weeks pay in our pockets to travel wherever we wanted. So the two of us slid the Buff's insignia off our uniforms and put our forage caps in our pockets and went to the station and bought cheap tickets for Pietermarietsburg. We didn't have the slightest idea where Pietermarietsburg was and we didn't really care. We loaded ourselves up with tins of condensed milk and bunches of grapes. They were dirt cheap. We travelled in a compartment with the blacks. We didn't think the Red Caps would look there. It wasn't very comfortable. It was crowded and the seats were wooden benches. Pietermarietsburg was a disappointment. It was getting dark when we arrived and there wasn't any nightlife at all. It was a religious community. They didn't look very favourably on us when we washed ourselves and our socks in the town fountain. We settled down to sleep beside the fountain but the bull frogs kept us awake all night long. We didn't want to stay there so Dennis hot wired a car, we filled our bottles with water from the fountain and set off. What Dennis had failed to check was that there was any fuel in the car. We went about fifty miles down the road and that was that. We had to get out and walk. We reached a village and settled down in a bar with the blacks. Then an Englishman approached us and asked if we were soldiers. There was no use denying it. Our army boots gave us away every time. He took us back to his house and gave us a meal. We had a real bath there. Then he took us to a station in his car, bought us train tickets for Durban and advised us to get back to our ship.

Durban was swarming with Red Caps (Military Police) and we knew that if they picked us up, we would be in real trouble. We made for the troopship but it was more difficult breaking into the docks than it had been getting out of them. There were guards on the gate - Red Caps! A native showed us the way, round the back and beneath the wire. We managed to reach our gangway without being stopped and reported to the ship's police. We were hustled up the gangway, questioned by the deck officer and put in the cells. We were sentenced to seventeen days field punishment and loss of pay. You couldn't do much about field punishment on board ship so we did fatigues instead. That was mostly peeling potatoes, mountains of them. We had to carry up supplies from the cold store, mostly potatoes. The quartermaster warned us to make sure the door didn't shut behind us when we went into the cold store. He also warned us about the rats. Despite the temperature, they thrived in the cold store and they'd grown thicker fur to cope with the cold. When we weren't working, we were returned to the cells at the back of the ship. That wasn't too bad because they left the doors open. They had to in case the ship was torpedoed. The cells were made of steel. We would have cooked if we'd been shut in in that heat. We had a pleasant breeze which was more than the others had in their bunks below decks and there was plenty to see, flying fish and birds following the wake and sharks. Some of the officers used to get on deck at night and shoot the sharks with their rifles. Then the C.O. sent for the defaulters. We were marched in left, right, left right, hats off, stand to attention. He told us he was going to rescind our sentences. We were only young lads and we would be going up the blue. He knew we would do our best. We still lost our pay though.

Then we reached Suez. We smelt it a mile away. The place stank but we weren't given time to look at it. We were marched straight to the station and on to a train, two hundred men at a time. There had been an outbreak of cholera in Suez and we didn't linger. I saw sights from the train that were a different world to me. There were plenty of Arabs and we soon learned that we couldn't take our eyes off them. They would steal anything.. They would wedge a lorry up with stones and steal the tyres. They would even steal the tents when men were sleeping in them. They were desperately poor. I had never seen hungry people before. Somehow theft didn't seem such a dreadful crime when you knew these people had nothing. We had to hand our rifles and ammunition in and they were locked away from the Arabs. The camp was guarded all the time but you needed eyes in the back of your head when you were on guard duty. The Arabs were up to all kinds of tricks.

We had become soft on board ship and now we were back to route marches in the heat of the mid- day sun. Then I was sent by train to Alexandria in a detachment of 25 men. We joined some similar groups from other regiments and were told that we were going up the blue. When the C.O. had used the phrase on board ship, I hadn't known what he meant but I soon found out. It was the Aussie term for the front line and it was soon used by everyone. The sky over the desert was a vivid blue which was deepest along the horizon in the west, where the fighting was taking place. We were being sent up as reinforcements and were told that we would probably be joining the Sherwood Foresters. That was bad news. The Foresters are a tough lot and the Buffs had had several fights with them. We went by train. At every station boys of all ages (wahlads) would walk along the train calling out eggs and bread. That is what they were selling, eggs in a large piece of bread like a bap. When we reached the railhead, we transferred to three tonners and went along the coast road. It was hot, so hot that we would take our boots off and dash into the sea to cool off. It wasn't long before we started to see signs of fighting and hear the sound of gunfire and the noise grew steadily louder. Our job was to round up P.O.W.s (prisoners of war) and get them back to the P.O.W.cages. We didn't have to worry too much about the Italians. Most of them had had enough of the war and were only too pleased to surrender. One day an Italian officer marched up with his men. He was one of the Alpine troops with feathers on his uniform cap and high, polished boots. He put his sword down with a flourish and surrendered the whole battalion. The men were smiling and seemed happy that they wouldn't have to fight any more. They were told where to go. We were passing groups of Italians all the time. We confiscated all kinds of things from them. I had a dozen watches that I wore on my arm and any number of fountain pens. They weren't any use in the desert but I sold them when I got back to Egypt. The Germans were different, especially the Afrika Corps. Even when they were prisoners they were telling us what they were going to do when they won the war. They weren't all arrogant, some of them were decent people but they were dominated by these others. When we rounded them up, we told them to throw their weapons and helmets down. If they didn't they were shot. There was no second chance. You couldn't trust them. We reached one place where there were proper water closets in the toilets. We'd only had holes in the ground until then. One of the men used the water closet, only for the whole lot to blow up when he pulled the chain. It had been booby trapped.

We had to keep the Italians and the Germans apart. They were supposed to be allies but they didn't behave like it. They would fight and there was a danger that they would kill each other. The tide had turned in the Middle East but the Germans weren't giving an inch. We were some way back from the front line and we didn't expect to be raided so it was a shock when we were attacked. We had a Bren gun mounted on the lorry on an ack ack mounting. As soon as we saw the German planes swooping towards us, we unhooked the Bren gun and drove off the road. They dropped their bombs. We knew they would be back. We had about ten minutes to reorganise ourselves when the driver in the lorry behind us started screaming for us to get the sand tracks. These were holed metal plates that we put beneath the wheels to give them some grip but in this circumstance they were useless. The officer was shouting at us to get the boxes out of the lorry. He wanted to lighten the load. The lorry was loaded with ammunition. My mate jumped into the lorry and started pushing the boxes towards the tail and I lifted them out on to the ground. Some of the others were running to help, when the German planes returned. Those that were out in the open dived on to the ground. There was a terrific explosion close beside us and my mate let go of the rope handle of the box and it fell on to my toes. We were lucky that time. No-one had been hurt except for me. My toes were broken. I was sent back to the First Aid post as walking wounded. The medics had plenty to deal with and I waited there for a couple of hours. Then the tent flap opened and I saw the blood and the wounded and I heard one of the men screaming and I knew I shouldn't be there, not with a broken toe while these men were so badly wounded. I hobbled back to my unit.

I saw some dreadful things in the desert, some that have haunted me all my life. I saw my first burnt out tank and went to see if there was anything to salvage. I climbed up the charred sides and there was the burnt remnants of a man, his head was bent down and one arm was lifted above his charred skull as if he had tried to escape. Yet there were beautiful things as well. When I think of those days now, I think of the beauty of it all, particularly at night. There would be noise and discomfort during daylight but a quiet settled on the desert when night fell. I liked to sit on my own, away from the others for a while. The sky was full of stars, thousands of stars. I'd never seen stars in London like those that shone in the desert and the dawns and the sunsets filled the sky with a kind of beauty I had never seen before. I would sit on my own and cover my cigarette with the palm of my hand so that the glow didn't show or stand there with an entrenching tool in my hand and wonder at the peace and the beauty of it all. That beauty could change with little warning when the winds blew and the sandstorms came with such ferocity that all one could do was try and seek shelter from the stinging, flying sand. Even the Bedou would lie down beside their camels for shelter.

There were two kinds of Arabs that we got to know, the fellahin, those that had little in life and the Bedou tribesmen. The latter were very proud people. They would come out of the desert with their camels. The first time we approached a Bedouin encampment, the driver stopped some distance away and waited. I couldn't understand why he stopped. After all, we had the gun but he waited for three minutes before he moved forward. That was to give the Arabs time to hide their women. Strangers were not allowed to set eyes on their womenfolk. The Bedouin would always offer water to any visitor. Water to them was a gift of God. They had five priorities in their lives, rifle and ammunition, (they were crack shots), Allah, water, women then tea or coffee. We often came across caravans of Bedouins with their camels some of which would be towing the black tents rolled onto long poles like sledges behind them.

Then the sergeant told us we were being sent back to Cairo for supply duties. We were delighted. Thoughts of a bath, sheets and women went through our minds, not necessarily in that order. We set off to the east the next morning by lorry. We were escorting prisoners, Germans. When we reached the rail head, we were relieved of our escort duties and told to climb aboard. They were flat bed trucks carrying damaged tanks that were being taken back to the workshops for repair. They were held in place with steel cables. We were to stand guard on them. The Arabs would have found something to steal even out of a damaged tank. There was only one covered wagon and the sergeant rode in that with the guard. It wasn't too bad in the heat of the day because the wind cooled us down but at nights, it was bitterly cold and we tried to sleep wedging ourselves in beside the tanks hoping that we would not roll off. It was a long, slow journey. We kept being pulled into sidings so that trains going west could pass. All traffic to the front was given priority.

We never did make Cairo. We went to Alexandria and were told to make our way to Ismalia, on the Canal Zone and we were there for two weeks with nothing to do. Mind you, we didn't have any trouble finding things to do. Our camp was beside the Bitter Lakes and we swam in them every day. I even made my way to Cairo one day and saw the pyramids. The camp was like a tented town. There were rows of tents as far as you could see and there were eight men to a tent so there were plenty of soldiers about. Then one evening, a senior N.C.O. called in the Mess tent and asked us if anyone wanted to earn a medal.

The answer was unprintable.

Then he asked if anyone wanted to go back up the blue.

Once again, the answer was unprintable.

Then he said we could avoid returning 'up the blue' if we volunteered. My pal said that it sounded a good wheeze so we volunteered and he told us to report for parade at nine o'clock the next morning.

There were men from all kinds of regiments there, the Jocks, the Green Howards, the lot. The Aussies had gone back to Australia by this time. They had put up a good show at El Alamein but the Japs were making themselves felt in the Pacific - Darwin had been bombed. The Australian government wanted their soldiers back. There were still some Canadians but mostly we were British. We were told that we had volunteered for the Parachute Regiment and anyone who wanted to drop out was to take one step forward. Nobody did. I didn't even think about it. I had been in the desert for a year. Anywhere else was heaven.

We went to the Parachute Training School at Kabrit. We had a medical but if we could stand up and breathe, we were passed. We did our first jump from a barrage balloon. That was hairy. There was no airstream to carry you out of danger if the rigging lines became fouled-up. Then we jumped from a DC3, through a side door. You would drop like a stone for ten yards or so. Then you would be pulled up with a jolt as the parachute opened. But it wasn't all jumping from an aeroplane. We trained hard. When we had completed our training, we had a cloth badge showing two wings to sew on to our right sleeve. I was in A Company of the 10th battalion of The Parachute Regiment. There was also an 11th battalion. Then we were joined by the 156 Para Bn (ex 151 Bn) trained paras from Rawpindi in India. They wore big bush hats that we envied. We had such an assortment of headgear from all our original regiments as the famed Red Beret had not then reached the Middle East.

Then we went to Ramat David in Palestine by train, through the Sinai Desert. There's only one way I can explain it all - bloody marvellous. Palestine changed my life. Religion had always played a part in my life. As children my sister and my three brothers had always attended high Church. Ever since I had joined the army, I had tried to understand other people's faith and religion. I had been fascinated with the mosques and the calls to worship in North Africa but now I was at the hub of the centre of Christianity and it affected me deeply.

One day, I walked down the 'Way of the Cross', the road that Christ had walked. It was a wonderful moment to me. I think that was when I decided to make something of my life. I'd been in plenty of trouble until then and I hadn't cared but now I began to see things in a different light.

Danny and I had been pals ever since we had joined up on the same day and he was Jewish. He spoke Hebrew and he was well educated. He knew things that I had never even thought about. One day the two of us were up in the hills. Rain water had collected in the hollows of the rocks and there were small worm like creatures wriggling in the pools. I was fascinated with them but Danny told me they were no good. They were the larvae of the mosquitoes that carried malaria. Then he told me about the insects and about malaria.

Another time, we were sitting in the hills, looking over Jerusalem and Danny said, "After the war, this will all be ours." I can still see him sitting there, saying it.

Danny was made welcome. He took me with him. I went to the synagogue. I didn't worship there but I was allowed to be present during their services. Then he was invited to a Kibbutz for one of the Jewish festivals and told that he could take a friend. It was a fantastic place. They had running water there. The land was irrigated and they were growing oranges and grapes. They gave us a sack of Jaffa oranges to take back to camp, big juicy oranges, not like the small hard ones we had had in the desert. Then there were the girls. They wore blue shorts and white shirts and they were smiling and happy. They drank wine at the festival. We had drunk beer but we'd never drunk wine before and we drank it like lemonade. We both stood up to leave at the end of the evening and that was the last either of us remembered. It was the first time I had ever been drunk I was careful with wine after that.

Danny and I often went to the Kibbutz. We were always welcome but there was one time when we were really appreciated and that was when we took them a bandolier of ammunition. The Jews were not allowed to have ammunition but it gave them a sense of security to have some. Even in those days, there was tension. There was an N.C.O. that got on our nerves. He always called Danny Yid and me, Chinky We got our own back We waited until he was on duty and stole his bandolier. We knew he would get into trouble for it and he did.. The elders at the Kibbutz asked if we could get some more ammunition and we managed to get them quite a bit one way and another.

Once Upon a Wartime X

We knew that we were going to see action at any time and we lived life to the full. We had leave at Haifa. That was another experience. We congregated in the evenings at The Brown Bear run by German Jews. We had some terrific fights there.

I was walking to the NAFFI when an officer called me over. He asked me my name and I told him, Pang. He asked me if it was pronounced correctly and I explained that everyone in the army called me Pang but the name had a different sound in Chinese. He then asked me if I could speak Chinese and I told him in the Mandarin dialect that my father was Chinese and my mother British.

"You've got me there," he said. "I speak Cantonese."

It was some days later that I was told to miss parade and report to battalion H.Q. I didn't know what it was all about but I realised I hadn't done anything wrong because the R.S.M. didn't knock my hat off so I was able to march in to the C.O. and salute. There were several other officers there including the adjutant and an intelligence officer. The C.O. asked me where I got the name Pang from and I told him, "From my father, Sir." He then asked me to speak in Chinese and I told him about my parents in Mandarin. There was a pause and he looked at the Intelligence Officer who nodded his head.

"Pang," the C.O. said, "you're in the wrong war," and they all burst out laughing.

"Blighty, here I come," I thought but it wasn't to be. I was given papers and travel warrants and told to be ready to leave the next morning. I was to make my way to Suez and report to the R.T.O. (Railway Transport Officer).

I reported to the officers and they would look at my papers and say, "Hang on here for a bit. Would you like a cup of tea?" before I was put on the next step of my journey. I joined the Troopship Arawa at Suez on its way to India.

I was fascinated with India from the minute I landed. There were so many different scenes and experiences. I couldn't get over the way they used camels in the same way that we used horses at home. Camels would pull loaded wooden carts through the streets of the town, quite at home with the congested traffic. But I found it dirty and dusty after the desert. The sun is a great purifier and, although the desert sand could be almost suffocating at times, it was clean.

I was ordered to report to General Headquarters at Delhi. I travelled by train and that was another experience. I met Major Jackman who commanded E group, an operational unit of M19. He was a great man. I would have done anything for him. He had earned everyone's respect. He had fought in the First World War and had a badly injured leg but he had taken over a small folding motor bike and he got everywhere on it.

"Good morning, sergeant," he greeted me.

That was the first I knew that I had been promoted and it was to take immediate effect. He told me to call in at the darzi wallah and get my three tapes put up. I met him three days later when my promotion had come through. At the same time, he had been promoted to Lieutenant Colonel.

I worked in the office for the first three weeks, learning the aims and purposes of E group. I had wondered what E stood for and I soon found out, escape and evasion. Captain Diwan Chand was the officer in charge and he taught me a lot. He held the King's commission. I had to understand about setting up and maintaining escape routes from behind the enemy lines. He showed me photographs of Japanese atrocities. He didn't need to tell me, I knew all about the rape of Nanking but all the same, I was shocked by the scenes he showed me. There was one instance where the Japs had caught an Indian soldier. They took his rifle and bayoneted him through his stomach with his own bayonet. Then they hammered it in so that he was crucified on a tree. Then they set fire to his hair and beard while they stood around laughing.

There were a number of stations behind Japanese lines that were manned by British officers. They operated portable radios, mainly 38s which they could strap on their backs. They were constantly on the move, never staying anywhere longer than two or three days. These agents often requested urgent military supplies and equipment and it was my job, travelling alone, to get these supplies delivered. Radio valves were the things that were most urgently needed. They were very fragile. We would wrap them in cotton wool and pack them into a condom, then put them inside a sock. We treated them like eggs. There were also constant requests for methadrine and water purifying tablets. It didn't take me long to realise that you never drank water from a stream when I went into the jungle. There were bodies floating in them and the local people emptied their waste into them.

The first job I did was to pick up three Burmese who had been in military employment. They had come along the ratline to the Assam border. A radio operator had sent a message to say that they were waiting collection.

I had my instructions. They were all verbal. I removed all signs of identification from my uniform, discarded my army boots, (they would have been a giveaway if I had been caught) and set off. I went by train to the River Ganges and crossed on the Golanda Ferry. The ferry was a paddle steamer and it took hours to cross the river. The Ganges was so wide at this point that you couldn't see the other bank when you set off. Boys were selling chapatis and bananas on deck and they became my staple diet when I was on a mission. I made my way to Kamila, the head quarters of the 14th army and went to the army cookhouse. It was the usual army meal, bully beef and potatoes washed down with an enamel mug full of sergeant major's tea, strong and sweet. I got my head down for the night, then I was ready for the next stage. I had a letter which I carried telling all army personnel to give me every aid to allow me to perform my duties. Nobody ever questioned it. I was shown a map and the area in which I would find the three Burmese was pointed out. I was told I could draw parts of the map in pencil but it was to be burned as soon as I had memorised the route. I had a guide to take me on the first part of the journey, but he was only allowed to come a certain distance. Then I was on my own. I travelled along tracks most of the time but hid in the jungle when I needed to rest up. The jungle is a world on its own. It was in the Monsoon and everything was wet and steamy. My shoes turned green with mould the first night. You can't see. The vegetation is so thick. You have to rely on your other senses. The jungle has all kinds of noises of its own and they took some understanding and so did the smells. I knew there were Japanese patrols in the area and I was alert for any sound that they made. Fortunately they were easy to distinguish and I would take cover in the undergrowth. I didn't smoke. British cigarettes have a distinctive smell and the smoke can travel along the ground for half a mile. Fortunately the Japs weren't so cautious and I would sometimes smell the smoke from their cigarettes before I heard them. I didn't leave any tracks or any litter. I hadn't taken any food with me. I ate in the villages when I could but that wasn't always wise. I had to be careful. Later on, I attended a course on jungle survival and learned how to find food but that was much later. I can't say I was frightened when I was left on my own but I was apprehensive. You never knew what you would find round the next corner. It was best to lie up during the day but it was difficult finding your way in the dark. I would take vitamin capsules with me and K rations.

It took me ten days to reach the area, then I had to find the radio operator. He could have been anywhere. I made my way to a native village. Not all the tribes were reliable. The Khasi and Lushai were on our side but there were others who were as likely to inform the Japanese of our presence. There were only men in the village but as soon as they realised I was English, the tension eased and the women and children came trooping out of the undergrowth. They knew where the Burmese were and I met up with them. They were pleased to see me. They all spoke English. They were men of the Burmese Rifles and there was no love lost between them and the Assam tribe that was sheltering them. One of them had a sawn off shot gun hanging from his neck by what looked like a piece of dressing gown cord and he wouldn't be parted from it. He didn't have any ammunition for it and the first thing he asked me was if I had any cartridges. Another had a Burmese dah, a dagger like sword which I would have liked but he wouldn't part with it.

We ate in the village but slept in the jungle. We never slept in the villages. I never did meet the radio operator.

We set off at first light and eventually reached Kamila. I went to the Sergeants Mess for a meal but the Burmese weren't allowed inside. I was scared that they would b. off but they were there waiting for me. I got them back to base. They had very useful information. We knew the Japs were planning to invade India and it was thought that they would come overland but the Burmese had seen them preparing barges.

It had been difficult getting the Burmese to the office. They had never seen a town before and couldn't believe all the sights.

My next job was to meet an R.A.F. pilot who was flying in from China. I was to go to Dumdum airfield. and take possession of a letter addressed to my officer. The pilot was flying in at night and on no account was anyone to know about my mission. It all went smoothly. The envelope was marked most secret. I duly delivered it to my officer. He opened it. There was another envelope inside also marked most secret.

"Oh well," he said, "you've brought it this far, you might as well take it on to Delhi."

I always had my own compartment when I travelled by train. That was a privilege that was generally only offered to officers. I had to show my pass and I was given priority. I was only supposed to go as far as Delhi with the pass but it opened all kinds of doors for me. I went through and met up with my brother in law on one occasion, first class treatment all the way. I would often go into the Great Eastern Hotel in Calcutta. This was for officers only but no-one questioned me. I was always in mufti and wore shoes. I wasn't the only soldier doing this job but I didn't know who the others were. I met up with a sergeant, Sergeant Kilops from the Black Watch on one occasion and realised we were doing the same thing. Then I had orders to go and collect his kit and return it to H.Q. There was only one reason I would be told to do that and that was that the sergeant had been killed. Then all his personal belongings were removed and returned to his family. I never knew what had happened to him.

Most of my orders were to deliver supplies into the jungle. I could travel at my own pace as long as I did the job. I was always wary, always listening out for the unexpected sound or smell. I soon became used to the sounds of the jungle but they could still be frightening, especially at night. I used the native tracks whenever I could and I approached the native villages but there were those I thought it best to avoid. The Japanese visited the villages regularly and I developed a feeling for their presence. It was the Japanese military police, the kempetai, that were most to be feared. They were responsible for a lot of atrocities.

One of the things I had to deliver were silver rupees. The natives wouldn't take payment in anything else. The first time I delivered them, I thought I was taking ammunition because they were packed in ammunition boxes. The rupees were packed in the box in cotton pouches. I was surprised when the officer took out the money. I got used to carrying it. On one occasion, when I was travelling by train, I had the box containing the rupees handcuffed to my leg.

I didn't sleep while I was going through the jungle. I would find a quiet spot and have a cat nap when I needed to rest but I could be alert within a second. I would be tired on the return journey and could report at any of the service camps and say, "I need to get my head down for a couple of hours," and everything would be provided, no questions asked. If any officer had any doubt about me, and I did look pretty rough sometimes, I would give them a phone number. They could call and they would be told that I was who I said I was.

It was difficult getting through the jungle in the monsoon. It rained so heavily, it was like trying to force your way through wet curtains and it was tiring. I would have to rest up. Then I would put the big gas cape over my head and settle down. My first inclination was to find a tree or bush for shelter but that would have been a mistake. Leeches were the bugbear of the jungle and they are attracted to heat, body heat. Leech bites went septic and caused lots of problems. There was only one way to get leeches off you and that was by burning with a cigarette end or with salt. Rock salt was as valuable to the natives as rupees and I often carried it with me. They even preferred rock salt to ammunition during the monsoon.

One of my orders was to get three jeeps with four drivers from India across to Assam. The drivers had never experienced anything like it before and they were scared stiff when we got into the jungle area. They were tank drivers but these jeeps were needed at the front line. They were loaded with supplies, mainly medical supplies and radio spares. I got them across the Galundo ferry and then took them towards the front line. We were in enemy territory and we had to be alert the whole time. We took it in turns to sleep as we were driving along but we only cat napped. The Monsoons had ceased but it was really muddy along the tracks and we had to avoid them from time to time. My orders were to deliver the consignment and get back to base but when we arrived, the officer wanted to keep me there and ordered me to stay. A soldier always has to obey the last order he has been given but my duty was to get back. I told him I would stay if that was his order as long as he told my senior officer why I had not returned. He changed his mind after that and I made my way back as usual. I made my way to the railhead at Dimapur. All supplies to Assam and Burma went through there. I reported straight to the R.T.O. and showed him my paper and I was found a place on the next train down to the ferry.

I never lost the apprehension I felt . If anything, I became more wary as I became more experienced. You could never know what to expect in the jungle. It wasn't only the Japs or unfriendly natives but the wildlife. Some of the insects were so poisonous, a bite from them could kill.

When I got back, Squadron Leader Elveston showed me a message he had received from General H.Q. in Delhi. I was to report to the British Military attache in Kunming, China. I was to report to the Great Eastern Hotel in Calcutta. That was the base for the civilian airlines. I had to take my belongings and report in full kit to the customs officer. My first thought was, "Why me?" but I soon found that out when I arrived in China. The Chinese didn't like the British managers or officers. In the past that class had taken big profits and caused a lot of trouble. The Chinese didn't forget. Tai Lee was the most powerful man in China, even more powerful than Chang Kai Chek and he brought regulations in that made it difficult for our officers to move around in China. It was a difficulty I didn't have. I had become dark skinned from being in India and I could pass for a native and often was. Even in India, I had been waved through checkpoints. In addition to this I had tattoos on my arms that were recognised by the Chinese and gave me entrance to places to which a foreigner would not be allowed. I reported to Calcutta and was given a ticket for Kunming. I was going to fly over the hump, the Himalayan Mountains. A coach took us out to Dumdum Airfield. Some of the passengers were British. The others were Chinese and American. We flew in a civilian aeroplane owned by the Chinese government, The Chinese Nationalist Airways Corporation, the C.N.A.C. We took off at midnight. It was dark as we became airborne but then the moon came out and we could see the land beneath us. We flew over snow covered peaks and miles of continuous jungle. The steward pointed out the wreck of an American plane beneath us. We saw several others as we flew on. We flew over the Chinese border and over the old Burma Road. The road showed up like a ribbon across the landscape, climbing up the mountains in a series of hair pin bends. We flew in darkness but then the lights came on and we were told we were on the approach for landing.

I was met at the airport by a White Russian called Vladimir Illen and he was great. He was tall and commanding and he worked as a civilian for the British Consul. He had plenty of other sidelines. He was a great character. He was fluent in English, French, Russian, Cantonese and Mandarin. He never spoke about himself but I learned that his family had escaped to China at the time of the Russian revolution and made their home there. He took me to his own home which was two rooms, made with clay bricks with a tin roof. It was situated just outside the North Gate by the river. The first thing he asked me when we got there was would I like a drink and he produced a bottle of rice wine. He drank enormous quantities of rice wine and said that it didn't bother him because he had been used to drinking vodka. We got on really well and spent ages sitting on our beds, yarning and drinking.

Vladimir took me in his jeep to report for duty at British Army A group. I reported to Major Don Sallinger. He was another character. He was Portuguese and had grown up in Macao. The senior officer, Lieutenant Colonel Ride was away at a conference. Major Sallinger arranged for me to have two weeks money in advance. He said that I would need it and told me to return at lunchtime to collect it and to bring a bag. I was paid in C.N. (Chinese National) dollars. I was given a pack of paper money and it was worthless. The locals wanted silver rupees or American dollars. There was nothing for me to do and he told me to report at nine o'clock the next day, so Vladimir took me round the town and put me right on a lot of things. That was the pattern for the next few days. I would report for duty at nine o'clock each morning and the rest of the day was my own. I got to know a country I had always considered my own. I can't explain my emotions or feelings when we landed at Kunming and it was a feeling that didn't leave me. It was bitterly cold. The only heating Vladimir had in his home was from a charcoal fire which he burned on a hammered out piece of steel which rested on a wooden cradle. One evening when it was the coldest I could remember, he stood up and opened the windows. I asked him what he was doing and he explained if he didn't do that, we could get really tired, too tired to move and then we would die. It was the first time I had heard of carbon monoxide poisoning.

There were plenty of American airmen in the streets paying for everything with American dollars. Vladimir had a good supply of those as well. One night I helped him pull a heavy trunk out from beneath his bed. It was fastened with two padlocks which he undid. The trunk was full of rice. I couldn't believe my eyes. Rice was currency. No Chinese wastes rice. Even as a child at home, we had not been allowed to leave a grain of rice on our plates.

"What have you got all that rice for?" I asked him and he simply told me that he had known hunger. Sometimes he sold it and bought fresh but he kept that trunk full of rice. While he was talking, he started running his fingers through the grain and I did the same and touched something hard. It was a World War One pistol and ammunition wrapped in oiled cloth. There were two of them. These too were currency.. He shut the trunk up again and pushed it under the bed. It was heavy. He had to keep it in the trunk as a precaution against rats. The rats were dreadful and could bring bubonic plague. I thought I had been inoculated against everything in the book but I hadn't been inoculated against bubonic plague. They would eat through the clay bricks. We could hear them on the roof. Rats were a part of China in those days.

Vladimir was killed in an air crash two months later. I missed him. I don't mind admitting that I cried at his funeral. It was pissing down with rain and we had had to pay a lot of money for the Chinese to dig a grave just outside their own burial ground. There wasn't a coffin. He was wrapped in a canvas shroud. There was no ceremony. He was dropped into the grave. Then one of the officers said, "They've dropped the b... the wrong way round," and they had. His feet were beneath the cross rather than his head but no-one was going to climb down into that hole and put him round the right way, not in that weather.

I inherited the tin trunk of rice.

One of my first orders in China was to collect a group from the north of the country. I was given two 3 ton trucks, two Chinese drivers and a Thomson machine gun - mine. We knew nothing about this group except that they would be coming along the rat line. We passed a lot of refugees coming towards Kunming. Anyone who had space in their truck or car could make a lot of money bringing people south. They were mainly women and children walking along the roadside, those that couldn't afford to pay. The Japs were advancing, pushing their way towards Kunming and people were desperate to get away.

We had agents that made arrangements to feed our own people that were travelling along the ratline and this is where we started looking for our group. We knew nothing about them at all except that they would be pointed out to us. The Japs wanted to take the airport because arms and supplies were arriving there for Chang Kai Chek. The atmosphere became tenser the further north we went. We were driving towards the Japs and knew that they already had spies in the area through which we were travelling. Even the drivers didn't know this area but they knew the road and that was a great help. We found our party in a Chinese village, a group of women and children. I don't think I can fully explain my feelings when I saw them. I had escorted men through the jungle, I had brought the Burmese out through Assam but these were harmless women and children, the youngest being just three years old. All I can say is that I suddenly felt incredibly humble. It was as if I had been given a God sent opportunity to help them. It was difficult at first because we spoke different languages. We spoke Mandarin and they spoke a rural dialect of Cantonese but, in China, although the different languages can be difficult, the writing is similar. These were people that had come from the same region in which my own father had grown up. It was over the next few days that I understood the reason for their rescue. Their husbands had joined the British Hong Kong Reserve Force. They were on our side. They had been specialist workers in the docks and their absence was causing problems to the Japs because they had no-one to immediately replace them. They had started taking their womenfolk in for questioning and that meant they were seldom seen again. Raping was only part of their treatment, even little girls weren't safe. These people had to be got out and it wasn't going to be easy. The Japs were very close. We started off at first light and drove almost continuously for five days. It was bitter cold but the Chinese were well wrapped up and they didn't complain. The looks on their faces when we reached Kunming was thanks enough. Of all the things that I did in the war, it was that incident that still haunts me. I brought twenty four to safety. There were many more that I couldn't help, innocent women and children.

The Yanks were pushing up the Burma road, repairing and making the road as they went. They used Chinese labour and they paid them, in dollars. No wonder the Chinese preferred the Americans to the English.

One day, an American sergeant with whom I was friendly told me that the Americans were six miles down the Burma Road and were going to enter China the following day. I knew that the sergeant was a member of the O.S.S. (Office of Strategic Studies) that afterwards became the C.I.A. and he knew what I did but we never mentioned it or discussed our work with each other.

I got a Harley Davison and went down to meet the Yanks. There they were polishing up their vehicles and themselves, ready to make the entrance the next day. A negro driver was fixing crossed flags on the radiator of his lorry, the K.M.T., (Chang Kai Chek's) and American. I stopped and spoke to him. I could

Once Upon a Wartime X

hardly understand a word he said and I think it was a good job the Chinese couldn't understand him either. Every other word was a swear word. Then the sergeant came up to see who I was. My head was shaved and I was wearing jungle greens. I had the wings of my para regiment on them. I could have been any nationality. The sergeant was suspicious and fetched his officer who demanded to know where the rest of us were. I told him back at the airfield and he nearly blew his nut. He calmed down a bit and it turned out that he thought the British had parachuted in and arrived in China before the Yanks could make their grand entry. It all sorted out and the next day went off exactly as the Americans had planned. The Yanks know how to make an impression. It was a fantastic sight seeing them come into the city, a day that no-one who was there will ever forget. The streets were lined with cheering people. The cloud of fear and depression under which so many had been living since 1937 was suddenly lifted.

It was August 1945 and the peace treaty had been signed but in China, the Japs refused to surrender to the British or the Chinese. They would only surrender to the Americans because they said it was the Americans that had beaten them. The Chinese were annoyed. It was their country. They executed a lot of their prisoners with a shot through the back of the head. That was the normal execution in the Far East and the Chinese have long memories. Their people had suffered atrocities from the Japs every bit as bad as those suffered by the Jews in the death camps.

My officer, Lieutenant Colonel Ride was ordered to fly to Hong Kong and take the surrender there but the same thing happened. He was told at the airport that the island would not surrender to him so he returned. The British navy weren't accepting that. They went in with a warship and a battalion of marines and the Japs surrendered Hong Kong.

Now we had to convince the Japanese that the war was over but a lot of them wouldn't have it. We had thousands of leaflets printed and they were dropped by air. I had to travel into different areas and make the announcement through a loud speaker but as soon as I shouted out the message, the Japs would shoot at me. I wasn't having that. I'd got through the war. I wasn't going to be shot in the peace. I made sure I was in a safe spot before I shouted through the megaphone.

I could have stayed on in the army. I was promoted to colour sergeant and then to R.S.M. I was to escort Japanese prisoners back to Japan and bring our own ex P.O.W.s (those that were fit to travel) back. But I had had enough. The war was over and the purpose for fighting it was over. I wanted to get home and make something of my life.

I was sent back to Burma to help guard a prisoner of war camp. That was an experience. The Japs resented being prisoners but not nearly as much as they resented the Koreans that were prisoners with them. They hated them. The

Once Upon a Wartime X

Japs could be cruel but the Koreans were worse and had been responsible for some of the worst atrocities in the war. The prisoners were given a supply of paraffin each day to light the lamps but they had been storing this in water jars. Then one day, they piled up their wooden beds and bedding in the middle of one of the huts, poured the oil over the pile and set light to it. Then they threw the Koreans on to it. The guards were Indians and they risked their own lives getting the Koreans out with the Japs trying to stop them. They had to use their guns and fire over the Japs' heads. When the Japs saw that the Koreans were surviving, the ring leaders ran into the burning building and threw themselves on the pyre and their screams as they died silenced the screams of the mob.

I returned to England on the troopship, H.M.T. Delware. I had a cabin to myself and no-one to tell me what to do. I was sent to Lilford Park in Northamptonshire to 7 CRU resettlement unit. Lilford Park was a beautiful old house and estate that had been taken over by the Americans during the war. Now we were preparing ex P.O.W.s to return for civilian life, giving them a future. Some of them had had horrific experiences. It was a completely relaxed unit at Lilford. There was no question of rank. We all lived as one unit. We all wore civilian clothes. What was important to me was that it was a mixed unit. There were women there. I met my wife there. She was in the A.T.S

One day a sergeant asked me what I intended to do when I came out of the army and I told him I didn't know. He had an application form for teacher training and none of the men in our care were ready for it. He suggested I applied. That was how I came to teach. It was tough. There was little money. I was married and our first daughter had been born but we pulled through together. In 1958 I faced the biggest shock of my life. My wife was taken ill and died. I had seen some dreadful things in the war, things I couldn't talk about even now but losing my wife was the worst thing I had even experienced. I had three children, the youngest just three years old and I couldn't cope. I went to pieces. I was in a dreadful state. If I hadn't met my present wife, I don't know what would have happened to me or the children.

Once Upon a Wartime X

Ron's mother and father

Sgt Ron Pang 6293195 in 'Battle Dress - Jungle Gree,' Posted from Middle East Command (Land Forces) to Far East (South East Asia Command)

24

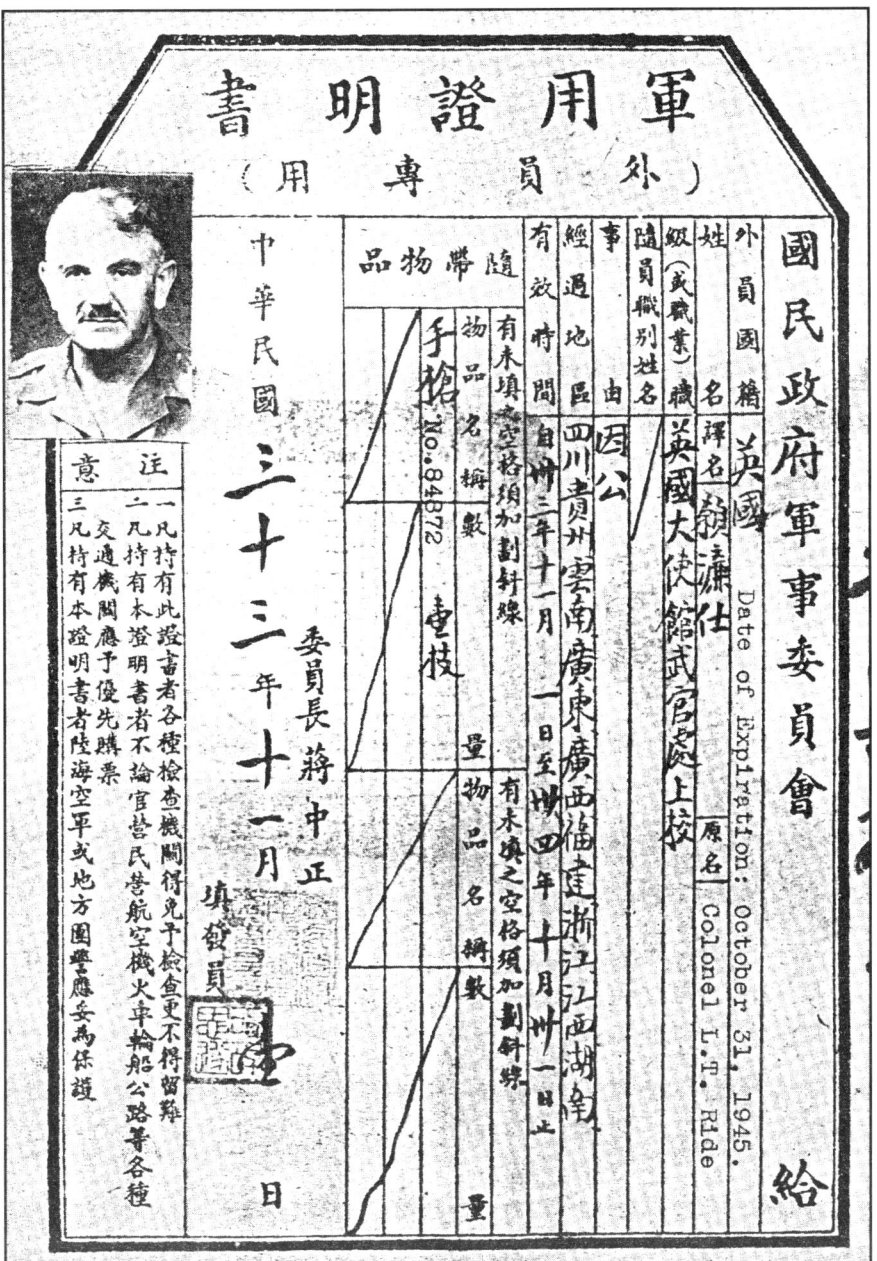

Certificate issued to Col. Ride by the Nationalist authorities. These passes were issued by local provincial governors and could take weeks to obtain.

APPENDIX "A"
to Scheme for Evacuation of
China Unit wives.

SOLDIER No.	Name.	WIFE, N A M E.	Children.	Others.
15001618	CHAN SIU TONG	NG KAM CHUK	1 son (age: 4) 1 daughter (age: 1)	
15001684	CHUNG WAI.	WU SIU HAN.	---	
15001676	FOK MING.	DAI SHIU.	1 daughter (age: 1)	
15001661	FUNG CHEUNG LUNG.	FOK YING.	---	Mother.
15001674	HO PUN.	NG LAI CHING.	1 son (age: 2)	
15001601	HO YAU.	LEE LAI WAN.	---	
15001596	HO YING.	CHAN YOK LAN.	1 daughter (age: 2)	
15001662	KWOK CHUEN FAM.	LIU KWAI.	1 daughter (age: 4)	
15001632	LAM CHO BUN.	WONG PIK YIN.	1 son (age: 6)	Mother.
15001605	LEE FAT.	CHEUNG WAI FUN.	---	
15001660	LEUNG KWAN.	IP SAU LIN.	1 son (age: 5)	
15001616	LEE KAY SANG.	LEE MO CHING.	1 son (age: 1)	
15001597	LO CHUN KIT.	LO WAI CHUN.	---	
15001584	MAK YIN JING.	FUNG SIN SUM.	2 daughters (age: 4, 1)	Mother.
15001863	TSE WAI.	CHEUNG TSUI KING.		1 brother of TSE WAI (age: 13)
15001866	YEUNG KEE.	SO TAI.	1 daughter (age: 1)	
15001608	LEW AH LOY.	WU SOOK SAU.		

This list was sent to us as the book was about to be published. These are the women and children escorted to safety. It is the first time he has seen their names.

WIRELESS OPERATOR/AIR GUNNER - Jim Taylor

I was the second of four brothers and we lived near Enniskillen. I did well at school and passed my school leavers Certificate when I was twelve and a half. There was no question of my staying on at school. My father bought some extra land so that there would be a farm for me to work but there were no buildings on the land and it needed a lot of cultivating. It wasn't for me. I went to Belfast and signed on for the R.A.F. as air crew, Wireless operator, after I had had a medical and taken a written test. It was July 1938 and I signed a nine year contract.

There were forty of us that set out for England. We'd signed on and taken the King's shilling in Belfast. We were kitted out at West Drayton and took the oath there. We did our square bashing at Uxbridge but some of them couldn't take it. They hadn't appreciated how unfit they were. There were a lot of people who hadn't had an adequate diet as children and didn't have the stamina. Some suffered from rickets and couldn't cope with the marching. There were others who couldn't face the regime and bought themselves out. It cost £20 and that was a lot of money in those days. There was one recruit who made out he was crazy and he was finally dismissed but he winked at me as he left the parade ground for the last time..

I went to Waddington to join 44 squadron. We flew Hampdens. There were four of us in the crew, the pilot, the navigator/bomb aimer, the wireless operator and the rear gunner. The last two looked out of the rear of the plane. It was very cramped and very cold. It was so cold that when I spilt some coffee one day, it bounced off my Sidcot flying suit as globules of ice. . We had detachable teddy bear linings for our flying suits and we had silk gloves to wear beneath our leather gauntlets. My friend took his off to unblock a gun and his fingers froze to the metal. He lost two fingers from frostbite. That was one thing about the war, they soon did something to warm up the planes.

We had an Irish officer on the station and he used to fly to Belfast on a Saturday afternoon. He'd always take some of us Irish lads with him. We had just flown over the Ladybower reservoir one day when I looked out of the window.

"Sir, sir," I called out. "We're flying over a nudist colony."

"So we are," he said and turned the plane round and flew over them at fifty feet, created quite a draft.

When we set off the next week one of the lads asked him if we were going to fly over the nudists. "Of course," he said.

War was declared on September the 3rd. 44 Squadron took off at 6.20 p.m.

Once Upon a Wartime X

We were to look for the German fleet at Heligoland and bomb it but we flew into low cloud and an electrical storm All we could see were the little blue lights of the other planes in the formation. Thank God we didn't find the fleet. We soon found out that bombers flying in formation were sitting ducks over warships. We brought our bombs back. There were the Naafi girls and the people from the village waiting to welcome us home. There was one plane missing. It had become detached from the formation in the cloud and came across the coast near Whitby and it was mistaken for a German. That was the first air raid of the war in Eastern England. We were just about to get into bed when the air raid warning went and we had to go to the air raid shelter. It was the only time I ever went in one. That was our lost plane coming back to base. We all swore at the pilot and let him know what we thought of him.

We were doing coastal command work, making sweeps across the North Sea, looking for submarines. Then we broadened the sweeps towards Norway, looking for the Altmaark. She was loaded with British prisoners, mostly from the Merchant Navy. A Blenheim Crew found her. Mountbatten went in and released the Britons. It caused an international incident at the time because Norway wasn't in the war then. None of the coastal trips counted as operations. We had to cross the enemy coast or territorial waters for that.

We knew the German codes. The Poles had got them across to us at the outbreak of war. The Germans sent out their call signs from their automatic stations along their north coast. They always started with three letters in morse followed by a long dash, they kept their finger on the button in other words. These three letters were changed every twenty four hours but we always knew them in advance. These beams could be set on specific targets and they were for the Luftwaffe to follow but we beamed in on them. I plugged in the loop aerial. In the Hampden, these wound down on the inside of the plane. I beamed in on zero and followed round until I found the call sign which I read out to to the navigator. He then plotted the position taking his bearing from where the lines of two call signs crossed. He had to take wind changes into account but he was accurate to within a mile. The Germans had no idea we knew their call signs and could not understand how we could be so accurate. We maintained radio silence as we crossed the North Sea. We had the short wave R.D.F. (Radio Direction Finding) which we could use in an emergency. There was a button we could press to destroy it if we ever ran into difficulties. We would approach the coast flying as low as we could to avoid detection. There were some raids where the bombers flew fifty feet above the waves. The navigator would identify the landfall when we reached the enemy coast and then we would aim for the target but the Germans could never be sure where we were going. We would often fly towards another town, then swing on to the actual target at the last minute. There were often several squadrons bombing the same target but they would come in from different angles which could add to the confusion. The path finders went in first and dropped flares so that we knew where to bomb. We always carried a couple of fifty pound bombs which we could drop at our own discretion and we never wasted them, especially when I was flying with Captain Smythe. There was one time we were returning from a raid when he caught sight of a train travelling towards France. This was round the time of Dunkirk. That would be a good use for one of our bombs and he swung the plane round but we lost it. Then he caught a glimpse of it going into a tunnel and we dropped one of the bombs in the entrance of the tunnel and the other at the exit so if they both went off as they were timed to do, the train would have been trapped. We maintained radio silence until we were within fifty miles of our own shore. then the pilot would tell me to switch on the IFF (Identification Friend or Foe) and then we really knew we were near home.

In January we were detached to Kinloss for a Norwegian tour. It was one of the coldest winters on record. We landed at Wick one night and stopped there for the night. When we woke in the morning, there had been a five inch fall of snow and we were snowbound. It was before the days of the tarmac runway. The C.O. got all the villagers and air crew out and anyone else on the base to stamp up and down in the snow until it had been made firm enough for us to take off.

Our next operation was to lay delayed action mines along the Kiel Canal They were primed to explode when the third boat went over them. It was some time afterwards that we discovered they only worked in sea water. We hadn't known that, neither had the Germans and they shut the canals for some time. We had flown so low along the canal that we had been flying between houses. We lost three Hampdens on that trip. We had been stood down on the 7th of Septemeber and were at the Theatre Royal in Lincoln. We were up in the boxes and we were all a bit merry. We were waiting for Phyllis Dixie, the stripper, to appear and there were plenty of catcalls to encourage her. Then the lights went up and the manager walked on to the stage. All airforce personnel were to return to their stations straight away. Transport was waiting outside the theatre and he started reciting the names of the stations, Waddington, Scampton, Helmswell, Digby.... Lorries (Garries) were lined up along the road outside the theatre and R.A.F. police helped sort people into the right vehicles. We were taken straight to the hangars and crewed up as we got into our kit. We had the briefest of briefings and then we were out to the bombers and preparing for take off. I was in the C.O.'s crew, Wingco Reid's. We flew out to Ostend at a thousand feet and bombed the barges that were loading up in the outer harbour. We dropped four 500 pound, seven second delayed action bombs but it was hairy. There was intense light flak and searchlights were lighting up the sky. We were caught in the cone of one of them and the pilot swung the plane from side to side in an effort to escape from it. Then he dropped down almost to sea level to get out of the light. We were hit three times, the last one in the tail and that made it difficult to control the plane's movement. I reached for the Verey pistol and fired a flare over the tail. That was how we lost the searchlight. They obviously thought we were on fire and started following the path of the flare and that was how we managed to get away from it. Despite the shrapnel and damage, the C.O. managed to get us back and land the plane safely. September the 7th. was the day that Hitler had planned to invade Britain. It was a day I shall never forget. The C.O. was awarded the D.F.C. for his part in the raid and he took the crew down to the Saracen's Head for a slap up meal to celebrate. It was the first time I had ever tasted champagne. I didn't like to tell him I would have preferred a pint of bitter.

I was late getting out to the hangar for the next raid and my pilot was standing there waiting for me.

"Where the hell have you been, Paddy?" he started.

I explained that I had flown in the C.O.'s crew to Ostend. He was furious and marched off to see him. He came back a few minutes later to say that the C.O. had told him to take someone else in view of the damage we had received at Ostend. He was going on that he had no need of an experienced wireless operator. He could find his own way over the drink. He asked me to kit out Sergeant Jones who had only arrived from O.T.V. that day which I did. I even gave him my parachute. That was my lucky day because that was one of the planes that did not return from the raid on Bremerhaven.

I was transferred to 207 squadron, the City of Leicester squadron, the first squadron to fly Manchesters and, once again, I was posted to Waddington. That was another lucky day. Bob Birt and I went into Lincoln on a motor bike to post letters home. Two girls were at the post box and we asked them where we could get stamps. We stopped and talked to them and asked them if they would like to go out with us. They refused at first, then they said they would meet us. That was how I met my wife. We were married for fifty- five very happy years.

We had three crashes testing the Manchester, well, two crashes and one shoot up over Driffield. We had broken cloud and were flying over an airfield when we were hit in a wing. I fired a Verey pistol in the colours of the day and the shooting stopped but we were furious at being shot by our own side.

Our first operation in the Manchester was to Cologne in February. It was a much heavier plane than the Hampden and we could fly higher. We hit flak as soon as we reached the enemy coast, pompoms that seemed to come snaking up towards us like oranges, getting quicker as they came near us and the heavy black balls of the shells that came at us in dark, menacing streaks. We felt the thuds as they exploded near to us. The whole plane shook and filled with the smell of cordite. There were other raids to Cologne, Brest and Hamburg. We would be flying for ten hours at a time. We all felt apprehensive at times and relieved when we crossed the English coast on the way home. The captain kept us informed about what was going on over the intercom and we communicated with each other in the same way. We had our flasks and sandwiches with us. We weren't allowed to smoke on board but we did, especially when we had completed a raid. I know I took a quick drag when I could.

We flew to Dusseldorf on the 27th of March. We had to make two runs over the city. It was a stupid thing to do but they were our instructions. We dropped incendiaries on the first run and heavies on the second, four times more than we could have carried on a Hampden. We had dropped our load and were on our way home when we hit. We had crossed the himmelbelt (searchlight belt) on the borders of the Ruhr. There was no flak then, just the German fighters. It was a fighter that shot us down. I didn't realise that we had been badly damaged. I felt a thump but we seemed to be flying steadily on. The first thing that happened was that the engine started heating up. I still didn't know we were in difficulties. I had seen tracer going by the window while I was on the receiver. I only switched to the intercom by chance in time to hear the pilot saying that he couldn't maintain height. He was down to 6,000 feet and still falling. We must bale out while we were still over land. I hardly had time to take it in before McDougal, the wireless operator, banged me on the shoulder as he dropped out of the turret. He already had his parachute on and he was gone before I had time to collect my thoughts. The navigator, Peter Gunnell, had already gone. The rear gunner had run all the way up from the rear of the plane. The hydraulics had gone on the rear turret and he wasn't able to get out that way. He was hard on my heels as I jumped. The hatch door was loose and floating around in the draught and getting in the way. I managed to push it to one side. The undercarriage was breaking away from the main part of the plane and swinging free. I was almost hit by the wheel. Fortunately I saw it coming and managed to dodge so that it only brushed the side of my face. Then I was falling. We had been told not to open the parachute immediately on leaving the plane and I think I fell a bit too far before I pulled the cord. Nothing happened. I almost panicked. I hadn't bothered to have it repacked for three months or more. I pulled again and it came out like a long piece of string. It was candling on me. Then it billowed out in front of me and, for a second or two, I thought I was falling upside down. Suddenly I wasn't falling. I was floating down and it was quiet and peaceful. McDougal was a little way over from me.

"Are you alright, Paddy?" he shouted.

"Fine," I shouted back, "how about you?"

We had time to look around as we floated down. I could see the fires of Dusseldorf burning in the night sky. I saw our own plane descending in a burning arc across the sky to end in an explosion as it hit the ground. The oddest thing about that night was that one of the two carrier pigeons we carried on board got back to base that day and none of us remembered releasing them.

The German fighter flew down beside us and dropped flares so that we could see where we were landing. We could see water. I knew we were over

Once Upon a Wartime X

Holland and I convinced myself that we were falling into the Zuyder Dee. I started inflating my Mae West straight away and I could see that McDougal was inflating his. I didn't roll myself in a ball on landing as we had been instructed because I expected to land in deep water. I stretched my legs out straight and landed in four inches of water and sprained my ankle into the bargain.

I released my parachute straight away, rolled it into a ball with the harness and waded to the edge of the water. Then I threw the package as far out into the deep water as I could. There was no sign of the others. I whistled softly but there was no answering whistle. I could see the plane burning and I started walking along a cart track away from the fire. I reached the village of Bakel. I walked along the village street and stopped to empty the water out of my flying boots. I was wet right up to my backside and cold as well. I threw my Mae West over a garden gate. The village was dark and deserted. I reached a pub, The Golden Lion, half way up the main street and went into the courtyard. A lighted candle was in one of the windows. I knocked on the door and, after a short while, a shutter opened. I said that I was an English flier. The door opened and I was whipped inside.. Fortunately the lady of the house spoke English so there was no difficulty with communication. I emptied my pockets and left photographs and personal things with her. She sent them back to me after the war. I gave her my Sidcot suit and lining and told her exactly where I had left my parachute and Mae West. I discovered when I met her after the war that she had retrieved them and made underclothes from the silk in the parachute. She fed me and dried me out. Then she made sure that I was setting out on the right road. I was making for a safe house in Utrecht, sixty kilometres away but I never got there. I was stopped by the village policeman. He took me back to the village and back to The Golden Lion and told them to report me to the Germans. He explained that if they had not done that, they could have got into serious trouble if it had been discovered they had sheltered me during the night.

Three German soldiers appeared half an hour later and marched me round to the barracks. They stripped me down to my underpants and put me in a bunk and I managed to snatch a few hours sleep.

They gave me my uniform back the next morning but the pockets had been emptied. Robson, the second pilot and Gamell, the rear gunner had also been picked up and the three of us were taken to identify the body of the pilot. He was lying not far from the burnt out plane. He was wearing his parachute but it had not been activated. The Germans checked it over and there was nothing wrong with it. It was thought that he had probably been hit by the propeller as he tried to escape because it was lying on the ground beside him.

We were taken to an aerodrome and we met up with the pilot who had shot us down. Sergeant Herzog was no Nazi. He was a thoroughly decent man. George Formason had joined us by this time and Sergeant Herzog gave the four of us a meal in the sergeants' mess. Afterwards he told us that regretfully he had to say goodbye to us and he meant it.

That evening, we were taken to Amsterdam by truck. I was still in a daze, still shocked by all that was happening to me. It all seemed like a bad dream. We were taken to a prison in Amsterdam that the Gestapo had taken over. We were stripped once again. There were five members from a Whitley crew there. There was a young ginger haired airman called Griffiths and a Pilot Officer Long. He was Jewish. He looked like a jew and he was scared stiff. He was disturbed and worried. I must say though that I never saw the Germans treat him differently from the way they treated other allied prisoners.

We were separated and put in cells with tall iron doors. We had to sleep on trestles, that was when we were allowed to sleep They kept waking us when we dozed off. Then they would take us into another room to interrogate us. They would give us a cigarette and pretend to be friendly but we knew we only needed to tell them our name, rank and number and we didn't answer any other questions.

We were there for three nights, then we were taken to the station under guard. We had to change trains at Utrecht and it was while we were waiting on the platform that Flight Lieutenant Shaw made a run for it. He had been the captain of the Whitley. He jumped down on to the railway lines and ran. The guards started firing at him. He would probably have got away if he hadn't tripped over a rail. The Dutch people crowded round the Germans stopping them shooting. There was a lot of shouting and threatening. It all started to become ugly. The officer came back and gave himself up. He had no choice.

We were taken to Dulagluft which was in the hills above Frankfurt. We went up to it on a mountain cog railway. This was a Luftwaffe Interrogation centre and they tried all sorts of tricks to get us to talk. They would threaten to shoot us if we didn't tell them what they wanted to know and we would hear volleys being fired outside but we only repeated our name, rank and number. That was all we had to do under the terms of the Geneva Convention. The Germans wanted to know more about the aeroplane we had flown. Our Manchester was the first they had seen and it had been smashed up on crashing. They didn't recognise the centre fin. They kept asking questions about it. But a few days after we had arrived at the camp, our C.O., Wingco Noel (Hetty) Hyde, had been brought in. He had been the pilot of the second Manchester to be shot down and his wasn't too badly damaged. The Germans were able to find the answers they wanted from that.

The C.O. walked round the football pitch with us, one at a time. It was the only safe place where we could talk without being overheard. He told me that he had written to my mother and said that he thought I had baled out safely. I was pleased he had done that. As it was, she didn't hear for another eight weeks that I was a prisoner of war. My name had been read out on German radio by Lord Hawhaw. He was an Englishman who had sided with the Germans and broadcast every night. It was all propaganda, German of course. He used to finish with a list of names of people who had been taken prisoner and that was how my parents knew what had happened to me.

In April, twenty of us were sent to Stalagluft 1 at Barth on the Baltic coast. This was a holiday camp compared with later experiences. The officers were in one compound and I was with the other ranks . We could volunteer to go out on work parties, to farms mainly. We had to give our parole but none of us tried to escape. We had been warned by the escape committee not to attempt to get away because it could have spoilt their plans but there was nothing to stop us collecting material and information for the escape committee. They made use of all sorts of things, odd pieces of wood or wire, pieces of paper. They particularly wanted parts of telephones and we became expert at dismantling the innards of a telephone in a few seconds when the opportunity arose. They wanted valves from radio sets, light bulbs and flex for the tunnels, magnets and coils. We would note where the roads were and find out where the station was situated. We also did our bits of sabotage, putting sand in the tractor petrol tank or cutting the tap roots of the lettuce so that they went to seed.

The guards weren't all Nazis. Our interpretor was very gentlemanly. He had some English but often made mistakes and some of the prisoners made fun of him although only a few of them made any attempt to speak German and when they did they made the same kind of mistakes that Herr Schreiber made.

We were taken down to the sea to swim on several occasions, always under guard of course. We received Red Cross parcels every week which helped with the food supplied in the camp. We were warned when we arrived to be careful of three British prisoners, one of whom was called Joyce and reputed to be the nephew of Lord Hawhaw. It was thought that these three were passing on information to the Germans. We were careful what we said in front of them. We had some French prisoners and there must have been a mole amongst them because one day, a group of us were rounded up, including most of the escape committee, and sent to a camp in Sudetenland. This was a dreadful place. There were all kinds of nationalities there, each in their own compounds, Greeks, Russians, Slavs, Croats. We were in a centre compound with Punjabis on one side of us and Russians, Slavs and Croats on the others. The Russians were treated dreadfully, worse than animals. Two carts drawn by mules would go into their compound every morning, one containing food and the other on which to carry out the bodies. The Russians would hide their dead for days on end so that they could get their rations. They were kept at starvation level. I've seen them rush the food cart and tip it over in their haste to get to the food, then they would be on their hands and knees licking it off the ground, they were that hungry. We tried to get some food through the wire to them when the guards weren't looking but we didn't have much to spare. The Red Cross parcels were still coming but we didn't get many of them. Most of ours went to the army.

Some of them had been prisoners since the beginning of the war and many of them had been captured at Dunkirk. Our basic diet was a loaf of bread between eight men, watery soup, weak tea and once a week we would have a spoonful of jam and some sugar but we did get the occasional Red Cross parcel and they saved our lives. We would have died without them.

Our hut was an old Czech barracks with a ceramic stove in the centre but there was virtually no fuel. We would shave off wood from our bed boards to have something to burn. Winter had set in and it was cold, bitterly cold, the coldest on record. We had wood chip mattresses on the bed boards and two blankets each but it wasn't enough. It was often too cold to sleep. We doubled up, sleeping back to back and that gave us four blankets but nothing could keep out that bitter cold. Then they took all the mattresses away and left them on top of hills so that we could see them. They did that as a reprisal because they said that their own troops, who had been taken prisoner in the desert, had been forced to sleep on the sand. The woodchip mattresses weren't comfortable but at least they gave us a little insulation from the cold. It had started to snow in November and we didn't see the ground again until April. There was one cold water tap between a hundred men and the toilets were holes in the ground above running water. I tried to keep occupied. I learned German and bridge. A Polish airman was my partner at bridge and we became fanatics of the game. Douglas Bader was brought in while we were at the camp. We all knew of his reputation and were quite excited to hear about him but we didn't see him. He was kept in close confinement and, at night, they took his legs away so that he couldn't cause them any more trouble.

The Croats and a few of the other prisoners were released. They were the ones who cooperated with the Germans. Then typhus broke out in the Russian compound.. They were taking out the dead every morning. Goering got to hear of the problems and he demanded instant action. The Red Cross was called in. We were all vaccinated in our chests. The next morning none of us could move our arms and we were moving round like a lot of apes. Our hair was shaved off and we were deloused. We were taken to the shower rooms and that was the first time I had seen the showers where two different pipes lead to the shower heads. I know now that one of the pipes contained gas but, at the time, I had no idea of that. Then we were sent to Stalagluft 3 and, believe me, after Sudetenland, it was like going to a holiday camp.

Stalagluft 3 was a brand new camp. We had sports equipment and materials with which we were able to build a theatre. There were two compounds there, one for the officers and the second for other ranks but we were able to mix for certain activities. There were still a lot of tree stumps and we were paid if we cleared them out. We were paid with lagergeld (camp money). I had my first letter from home and one from my girlfriend. I don't think I can put into words what that meant to me. Some of the poor devils had Dear John letters. We used to make a joke about them and put them on the wall but they weren't funny to the people who received them. People at home didn't seem to understand what the conditions were like in a P.O.W. camp. One lady wrote to her boyfriend and said she hoped he wasn't seeing too many German frauleins. We could receive four personal parcels a year but I only received three in all the years I was a prisoner although I knew they were being sent to me regularly. We rationed out the things the Red Cross parcels contained. We missed cigarettes and tried smoking all manner of things, rose petals and tea leaves but they were foul and that was when my friend and I decided to give up smoking.

A crew from a Wellington were brought in one day. They each received a Red Cross parcel containing five hundred cigarettes and a bottle of whisky that the Germans took. It turned out that they had crash landed on a railway line. The rear gunner broke his hip in the crash. The pilot sent one of the airmen back along the line with flares to set off and stop an approaching train, which he did successfully. The Germans appreciated that they had saved a lot of lives by doing this and were considerate towards them. Goering got to hear what had happened and when he heard that they hadn't received the whisky, he ordered that they had it immediately and they did. What was more, he told the British that the pilot should be awarded a medal for his actions. He received the D.F.C. and the rear gunner the D.F.M. We had an escape committee and we were on the look out for anything that would be useful to them. One day a German guard was repairing a fence and he laid his tunic on the ground. We were into action straight away. We surrounded him and kept him talking while one of the P.O.W.s sneaked his passes out of his pocket and they were away to the forger. When it came time for the guard to go off duty, he picked up his tunic and went mad when he found his identity cards and passes were missing. He drew his gun and I think he would have shot us but we calmed him down. We pointed out that if he waited a while, he would have everything back but if he went and reported us and made trouble, he would be charged for losing his papers and that was a serious offence. He saw reason in the end and calmed down and both sides were satisfied. Well we were anyway.

We could see the railway line from the camp in Sagan and we would watch the hospital trains coming from the Russian front. We knew what was going on because we always had a wireless set in the camp. Some components came in parcels. Others were made by the men. The Germans were always trying to find where the wireless sets were hidden. We kept ours in an accordion. The accordion still played and the Germans never suspected or wondered why this officer carried an accordion with him everywhere he went.

The escape committee had started activities as soon as we moved into the camp and when we were moved on, we left an almost completed escape tunnel to the Americans.

We were marched down to the station and loaded on to cattle trucks and we were in them for four days and nights. There wasn't enough room to lie down. We could see where we were going through the slats. We were pushed into a siding at Potsdam and stopped there for ages. We were there when there was a raid on the town and all the Germans disappeared and we were left like sitting ducks locked in the cattle trucks. It was a frightening experience being on the receiving end of an allied raid. There were slits high up in the trucks that acted as windows and two of the men in our truck, Flight Sergeant Nobby Hall and Sergeant Linley, managed to wriggle through one of them when we were going through a marshalling yard but they were recaptured a month later.

Our destination was Stalagluft 6 and it was alright at first. The Poles were segregated from us so my bridge partner, Marion Przybylski, was in the other compound. The Germans were getting jumpy. Things were not going well for them. The Russians were advancing steadily and there was talk that we would be home for Christmas. "Good old Joe (Stalin)" was our battle cry. We were communist to a man.

The Germans were getting really jittery. They started moving us out but they were cruel with the first group. They made them run. After four years in captivity and with the poor diet, the men were in poor physical condition.

Then it was our turn. We were marched to the station and loaded into cattle trucks again. We were taken to Fallingbostel 357, a camp that had been occupied by Russian prisoners. 15,000 Russians had been there but only 400 left. A few Russians were still at the camp. They had been kept to do the menial jobs. The officers reached an agreement with the Germans to let us have a shower once a month. These showers were similar to the ones that we had at Sudetenland. There was a Russian sweeping the floor. I had a little Russian and he had some German so we managed a conversation. He pointed out the shower heads. "Wasser," he said. Then he pointed at another and said," Gas." I realised the significance of those pipes then. There had been no gas in the Luft camps.

Things were stark in the camp. There was very little food but it was the same for the Germans as it was for us. We didn't have any winter clothes and memories of that first winter I had spent as a P.O.W. still haunted me. Then I had a stroke of luck which I reckoned could have saved my life. I received a parcel from a cousin in Canada. It seemed their son was in the airforce and he had told them what to send. There were two sets of winter underclothes and a thousand cigarettes. I gave one set of underclothes to my pal, Harry Logan, and we put them on straight away. The cigarettes were a different matter. We had given up smoking and those cigarettes were a big temptation to start again but, at that stage of the war, cigarettes were more valuable than money. We spent days looking at those cigarettes, wondering what to do. The men in the hut made plenty of suggestions but in the end we decided that it would be silly to start smoking again. It was a good job we did. We used those cigarettes in exchange for food.

There was an elderly guard that was on duty every Friday night. We weren't allowed to communicate with the guards but I managed to make him understand that I would pay him 18 cigarettes for a loaf of bread every time he came on duty. His mother was Czech so he was more sympathetic towards us than the other guards and he agreed to help. He would nod at me when he came on duty on a Friday evening so that I knew he had a loaf. I waited until it was dark and timed my escape from the hut until the searchlights had swung over our patch, then I would slide out of the window and run towards the fence. The guard threw a two kilo rye loaf over the wire and I slid eighteen cigarettes which I had put in a tin box under the wire and waited until he slid the empty tin back. Then I would pick up the loaf and make for the hut. It was a close thing, getting back through the window before the searchlight came round again.

Two Russians came into the camp each week to empty out the cess pits. They came on a horse and cart which was driven by a Hungarian driver in a German uniform. I had a little Russian and I asked them if they could bring some food in for us. They agreed to bring a cabbage or some onions each time they came and I paid them two cigarettes each for them and seven cigarettes to the driver of the cart because he was the one who hid the vegetables beneath his seat. They were taking a dreadful risk in helping us but I'm sure that extra food helped us to survive.

We were following the news avidly and getting excited about the allied advance. The last news we heard was that they had reached the Weser and had built a pontoon across the river at Munden when the guards suddenly announced that the camp was being evacuated. Eight hundred of us were lined up and marched out of the camp. We were mostly airmen and Irish Guards. We marched north and spent three days crossing Lunenburg Heath on cart tracks. They kept us away from the main roads. Some of the men made a run for it as we went through wooded areas but I don't think many escaped. The Germans shot them down with Sten guns. Each night we were counted off in hundreds and shut in sections of a farmyard. Then the Germans came round with the food cart and we were given a loaf which we had to share between four of us. There were two carts accompanying the march, one to carry the sick and the other which contained the food. There were plenty of sick. Some of the men were very weak. As we walked along, I got to talking to one of the guards. He was older than the others, probably in his forties. In peacetime, he was a Shakespearean actor at the Hanover Opera House. He had no interest in fighting or the war. As it happened, I had studied Shakespeare at school and we had had to learn a lot of quotations. I would quote something to him in English and he would quote something in German. So we marched along quoting Shakespeare at each other. We marched about twenty five miles a day and I asked him where we were going. He said he thought we were going to Denmark and probably on to Norway. We were being used as hostages.

That was a shock. We knew the war was drawing to an end and all our thoughts were of getting back home. I'd been in captivity for four years and I had had enough. I was going to make a run for it but the German guard advised me not to. He said I would be shot. That was their orders and although he had no intentions of killing anybody, there were certainly others that would.

"There's a better way than that," he told me. "When you are shut in the farms at night, you have ten minutes before the guards are put round the site. If you can get away in those ten minutes, you have a chance to escape."

I discussed the situation with Harry and the two of us worked our way up to the front of the column so that we were in the first hundred to be detailed off that evening. We were shut into a yard with six foot walls and a wicker gate that led into a wood store. The logs were packed in tight but I worked my way round them and found another gate leading into a straw barn. This was our way out. We didn't wait for the food to be distributed. We jettisoned everything we were carrying except for our coats and blankets. We had to travel light. We made our way out of the buildings and hid behind a privet hedge. We crouched down and waited for it to get dark but then we heard dogs barking and knew they were setting up the guard, There was no time to waste. We ran, crouching as low as we could and made for a pile of straw on the hillside and hid behind it. We only just made it before the German guard took up their positions about fifty feet closer to the farm than we were. We had made it. We waited until it was dark and made our way into the woods.

We travelled at night and lay up in the woods during the day. We drank water from streams or pools and within two days we both had dysentery. We'd been walking for five days when we had a stroke of luck. We came across a group of Italian P.O.W.s working on a farm. I didn't speak Italian but I had some Spanish so, with that and some German, I made myself understood. We swopped our coats for their Italian cavalry coats and caps. Now we looked less like British airmen. The Italians advised us to go to the east rather than continue the south west route we were taking. We were near the town of Saltau and there were a lot of Germans there. It was very foggy the following night and we couldn't move very far. We settled down for the day near a farmhouse. There was a peat store between us and the farmhouse similar to the one we had on our farm at home. We found our way into it and settled down to sleep on the peat. It was drier and warmer than the open ground. We could hear ducks and I knew this farmer was doing the same as we did at home in Ireland. He kept his ducks in runs beneath the peat. Before daylight, we made our way to the ground and went round to the other side of the shed. Sure enough, there was the door where I expected to find it. It was only a small door but I wriggled inside it while Harry stood guard. I knew ducks lay their eggs in the corners and I managed to collect fourteen and hand them out to Harry. Then I told him to keep the door shut firmly so that it was completely dark inside. I felt round until I caught hold of a duck and I necked it. It was a big, fine, white duck. We made for the woods then and sat down and studied the food we had found. I broke open an egg and ate it raw but Harry couldn't bring himself to do so.

"Look," I said, "you can't afford to be squeamish. You eat this or you die."

He managed to swallow the raw eggs but it took a big effort on his part. Then I cut the duck open. There were some more eggs inside, one of which was ready to be laid. We ate those as well and the liver and heart and kidneys. We even tried eating some of the leg but neither us could stomach that, so I hid the remnants of the duck under some leaves and we went on. As dawn broke, we were sitting on the bank of a main road, wondering if we could risk crossing to the other side when a German convoy came into view. We didn't have time to hide. We carried on sitting where we were. There was nothing else we could do. I could see the German general in his staff car studying us through his binoculars. As he came abreast of us, we waved and they drove on. We thanked God that we had the Italian uniforms on. Had we still been wearing our airforce greatcoats, we would have been captured for sure and probably shot.

When we did get across the road, it didn't help because we found ourselves wallowing in a swamp. We sunk into mud up to our knees and it was an effort to get out of it. We were sitting recovering with our backs against a tree when we saw the planes flying over and then the bombardment started. The allies were bombing Saltau. They were dropping blockbusters and the ground shook beneath our feet. Shells were flying over our heads. There was no way we were going to move while that was going on. We stayed hidden. In the early morning we heard diesels starting up and we knew we were near German tanks. About six o'clock in the morning, we saw smoke curling up and we could see the outlines of a farmyard. Harry stayed hidden while I worked my way down to it. We had to find out what was happening. I saw a young boy, obviously one of the forced labour workers, come out of the buildings to relieve himself. I whistled. It gave him such a shock, he wet himself, but that didn't bother him overmuch. He explained that the Germans had started to move out during the night and that they had seen British tanks the morning before but they had retreated again. There were still German troops about but he urged me to fetch Harry and hide in the barn. By the time we returned, he had a ladder against the wall and we both climbed into the hay loft. There were two of these boys now. They were both Polish slave workers about fifteen years of age. They climbed into the loft after us and covered us with hay. A couple of hours later we heard the ladder being put against the wall and a young girl of about fourteen clambered across the hay. She had brought us food, a roast duck and a bottle of cherry brandy. It was the first cooked food we had had for days and it smelt good but after we had eaten, we were both violently sick. Our stomachs couldn't take it.

We stayed hidden in the hay and then we heard a commotion in the farmyard and a lot of shouting. It sounded as if our new friends were in trouble and we hurried to join them. A German sergeant was against the wall and he was threatening the young people with his rifle but the four of them, there was a second Russian girl, had him cornered with pitchforks and were screaming at him.

We tried to calm them down. The German had been wounded and he was like a cornered animal but he listened to sense. I suggested we came to an agreement. We didn't know who was going to find us first. If it was Germans, would he see that we were alright. If it was the British, we would look after him. He was relieved at the suggestion and sat back against the wall. He tore the sergeant's stripes from his uniform, broke up his rifle and threw the pieces away. He wanted me to take his pistol but I told him to keep that. If I had been picked up by the Germans with a weapon on my possession I would have been shot. The two Russian girls weren't keen on the arrangement. They hated the Germans and they hated the gauleitier in the city more than any of them. They could see their way to paying him back for the way they had been treated. They had both been horse whipped and they had great weals across their backs. They were ready to set off then and there to pay this man back but we persuaded them to go and prepare some food. They had milk and they had eggs.

In the afternoon we saw a German soldier staggering in the fields. We thought he was drunk and one of the Polish boys went out to fetch him in. He was a German youth. I doubt if he was more than fourteen years of age. He was completely shell shocked and he was shaking uncontrollably. He didn't know where or who he was. He'd been in a fox hole while the battle had been taking place. These lads had been put on their own in these fox holes and told that they must die for the Fatherland. We managed to calm him down and the German sergeant spoke to him gently but it was some time before he stopped shaking.

It was about this time that two Canadian airmen that we had known in the camp came into the yard. They were fit and in better condition than we were. They decided to push on and not stay with us. They would have done better if they had because they were never heard of again. When we had returned to the U.K., we were asked if we had seen them and we explained how they had left us in the farm. We were the last people to see them.

Meanwhile the other Polish boy had slipped out to find what was going on. He'd worked his way along the ditches and when he returned he said he had contacted the English and they would be coming for us. It was late in the evening when three armoured vehicles came along the lane. Harry and I burst out cheering when we saw them and would have run out to meet them but a voice boomed out telling us that they were the British army and if there were any allied troops inside, we were to go out with our hands up. We went with our hands in the air and grins on our faces. It was the Red Caps, the Military Police, that had come to fetch us. There was no nonsense with them. They were hard and they were tough. They wanted to know who everyone was. By this time the farmer had emerged from the farmhouse and was sitting on the doorstep sobbing. He thought he was going to be shot. The men asked if he had been any trouble but we said he hadn't. He must have known we were there but had done nothing to harm us. He was left. They asked about the German and we explained that he also was no trouble and neither was the young German boy. They were both put in one of the armoured vehicles and taken back to the camp with us as were the two Polish boys. They were pleased to come. The two Russian girls were invited to join us but they were already leaving for the town before we left. They went in search of the gauleitier. They had a big score to settle with him and they could think of nothing else.

Before we left, the soldiers went and shot some pigs and loaded them into one of the vehicles. They took some hens and eggs as well. Then one of them went up and paid the farmer with a handful of German marks. The farmer seemed satisfied and we left him still sitting on the step as we drove off. There was no nonsense with those soldiers. They were tough, hard men.

They took us back to Stalag 357. There were no guards there now and the gates were open. The whole area was packed with people, people of all nationalities. We were deposited at the gate, given some iron rations and left. They told us that as soon as it was safe enough to get over the River Weser, we would be taken out of the conflict zone. Meanwhile we waited in the camp. The two Polish boys melted into the crowd and I never knew their names. The two Germans were taken on to another camp. The two of us went back to our old barrack block, put a couple of mattresses on the floor and settled down to wait. There were other P.O.W.s there who had either escaped or had been marching from the east, some of them for months. Besides the British, there were Americans, Poles, Russians, British Commonwealth servicemen. Some of them had escaped from the Germans and then the Russians. There were still some of our old escape committee there. There was a right motley crew.

The next morning, a group of us set out to raid the silos which towered on the edge of the town. There was a queue climbing the winding stairs to the top of the grain store and another trying to stagger down with bags of maize, wheat and rice. Some of the starving looters threw sacks out of the hoist doors. They were exploding on the ground and the contents being scooped up by the people waiting there. There was no question of anyone being an enemy of the other, we were all trying to get food. There were plenty of Germans in the crowd and they were amazed that there was so much food stored there because the rations they had been receiving had done little except stave off hunger.

There was a cache of boxes on the top floor, boxes and boxes of fountain pens, ersatz coffee, glucose tablets, Eau do Cologne and other things that had obviously been reserved for the Gestapo. I brought a few samples of the goodies home with me but our main priority was finding food and getting it back to the camp.

The inevitable happened. Looters began fighting amongst themselves and someone set fire to the sugar and grain on the sixth floor. The fire died down after a while but we had plenty of grub to see us through the next few days.

Then the British troops arrived. They came with fixed bayonets and they weren't gentle. They had a terrific problem sorting out the genuine refugees. Some of the guards and soldiers had thrown away their uniforms and claimed to be refugees. We allied P.O.W.s identified ourselves and they were alright with us. We all had our identity discs. Harry and I had hidden ours in our shoes when we had escaped. We knew we mustn't lose them. Army trucks eventually came. We really began to feel we were going home then. We crossed the River Weser at Minden on a pontoon bridge. All we could think about was home. We went to Rheine Airport where R.A.F. Dakotas of transport Command were waiting. About two dozen of us were loaded into each plane and taken to Schipol. I can't remember how we got to the Belgian Army Hospital in the Rue do Roi but that was where we finished up. All our clothes were removed and taken to the incinerators. We were deloused and then kitted out with army uniform. We were issued with two hundred cigarettes each and some other goodies and mugs of hot, sweet tea of course. It was good to be alive I weighed two and a half stone below my normal weight but there were some that were in a far worse condition than me.

Our next stage on the road back to Blighty was being flown in Dakotas to R.A.F. Wing in Bedfordshire, then by night train to the Rehabilitation Centre at Cosford. We had medicals over the next few days and then leave, as long as we could be near a R.A.F. medical team. Harry set off straight away for his home at Stockton on Tees and I made for Lincoln to my girl.

I stayed with her parents and attended the Sick Bay at Waddington until my chronic dysentery stopped. I had been suffering from it ever since the first day of our escape and I didn't think it would ever clear up, but my fiancee's uncle had the answer. He mixed brandy with the whites of eggs and that did the trick. I then went home to Ireland for two weeks and my mother set about feeding me up, eggs, fresh cream, home cured bacon. I put on nearly a stone in a fortnight. I returned to Cosford for further medical care and we were pampered. There was plenty of food and plenty of exercise. Then I was posted to Wittering but first I had more leave and I married my sweetheart. Harry was my best man. A few weeks later I was his best man when he married his girl friend.

I returned to Wittering and remustered as a wireless/radar mechanic. My C.O. advised me to complete my nine year contract. He said that would give me time to make sure I was completely fit and I took his advice. I was posted to Linton on Ouse as a warrant officer in charge of the Radar section. There was little flying by then and my job was mainly supervising WAAFs dismantling old radar equipment. In 1947 I was asked to apply for a commission but I turned it down. Financially, I couldn't have been better off. Our son had been born and we had a married allowance on top of my pay. But my wife didn't want to move around and I was ready to settle down, besides I had been accepted for teacher training. My wife stayed with her parents while I went to college. Then I took a post at St. Giles School and I stayed there for twenty two and a half years finishing up as the deputy head. I was also the tutor organiser for the Borstal in Leicestershire. I had my home and my family. I was and am content. I wouldn't wish the captivity on anyone but the war gave me the opportunity to achieve these things.

Hamden Z 1940 44 (B) Sqdn, Waddington

Uxbridge August 1938

GALLIPOLI - Robert Street

MY GRANDFATHER, ARTHUR STREET, DIED IN AUGUST 1970. I DON'T REMEMBER A LOT ABOUT HIM, BUT WHAT I DO, I REMEMBER WITH FONDNESS. WHEN I WAS ABOUT FIVE OR SIX I'D SIT ON HIS KNEE WHILST HE DRANK HIS 'DAVENPORTS' AND TOLD ME STORIES OF THE GREAT WAR. I NEVER FORGOT THEM. HE WAS IN GALLIPOLI, TURKEY. THIS IS HIS STORY:

I was born in April 1891. My parents were working class, as were theirs before them. In those days if you were born working class you stayed working class. There wasn't any football pools then. Dad worked in a factory as a steel toy maker. Money was tight but we didn't starve. The old man saw to that. We lived in one of the old back to back houses in Miles Street near the city centre of Birmingham. I left school at fourteen and went straight to work. I took a job as a bicycle mechanic and then as an apprentice stonemason, but couldn't settle. Whatever I did it seemed that I would be trapped in the working class rut, living the rest of my life on the breadline and I didn't fancy that. I decided that I wanted to see a bit of the world and maybe somewhere along the way I might get a lucky break. So I joined up, the 4th Battalion of the Worcestershire Regiment. I was only nineteen, but had no ties, so I thought I'd give it a go. They were based at Norton barracks in Worcester and that's where I did my training. It was hard there, but I was used to hard work so didn't mind and we were kitted out, fed and boarded. I think some blokes were just glad of that and to have a roof over their heads and regular meals. It was there that I used the Vickers machine gun, becoming quite a crack shot.

In 1911 I took part in a grand parade in London. We were 'dressed up to the nines' in our smart uniforms with tunics and fancy helmets. I really enjoyed being part of the pomp and ceremony. I could never have done anything like that if I had remained at home.

Shortly after we were posted to India, in the Central Provinces and later to Burma. That was a real eye opener. The colonials out there lived a life of luxury whilst the locals lived in poverty. Of course we loved it, peacetime soldiering in a place were the King's shilling went a lot further than at home. We had servants or dhobis as they were called to attend our needs. They changed the sheets, washed our kit; one of them, shaved you in your bed if you wanted and all for a few annas. In the towns it was just as amazing. Street magicians and traders of all sorts descended on you to perform some trick or sell you something and it was so cheap too. One man put a knife through the back of his neck and you could see it moving by his adams-apple. Then, he removed it and not a mark could be seen. We couldn't believe our eyes, but it happened.

Peacetime soldiering wasn't a bed of roses though. We worked hard keeping the locals in order and chasing bandits. We did have some free time, but there wasn't any real social life for us soldiers then. The colonials were all right, they had their clubs and parties. Most of us had a hobby to fill the time. Many took up carving and produced some beautiful figures such as elephants and tigers to remind them of India. I took up butterfly and moth collecting. I was in the forest one day and looked at a brown leaf that appeared to have snow on it. I went to touch it and it flew away. It was a large moth; I was amazed. It was then that I decided to catch them for a hobby. I obtained some mosquito netting and wire and cut down some bamboo and I was away. I caught hundreds of all sorts of colourful and exotic types, later mounting them in glazed frames. After the war, when money was tight, someone said they were worth quite a bit, so I sold them. A chap in America said he would buy them and I sent them off. He never paid me.

During one of my excursions into the forest I heard a noise behind me. I thought it might be a bandit so cautiously carried on. Whilst pretending to be examining some foliage I took a crafty glance over my shoulder. I suddenly froze. It was a tiger. It was peering from behind a tree, weighing me up. Mind you, I must have looked strange in my old style uniform with sun hat and leather spine pad down my back. I think it was only a young one because it didn't seem fully-grown, but it was big enough to sort me out. I wasn't too far from the camp so decided to make my way back, waving the large bamboo pole with the net on as I went. This young tiger stalked me virtually all the way back, but I think the pole put it off fortunately for me and I was relieved to get back to safety. On another occasion whilst tramping through the undergrowth I disturbed a water buffalo. It wasn't pleased at all. I think it may have been a mother protecting its young. Anyway, it came after me and I ran as fast as I could. I ran towards a steep four-foot bank with this snorting animal chasing after me. I jumped up the bank and onto the track above, just as the beast got close enough to spin round and kick out with its back legs before scurrying off. If it had caught me it would have certainly broken my legs and it would have probably been all over for me. An injured animal of any sort doesn't last long in that environment. There was plenty of wildlife about then and we didn't frighten it either. Many a time hawks would snatch grub from your plate and even cheetahs snatched dogs from leads when people walked them down the forest tracks.

We travelled by train where we could. I remember getting off the train at Bareilly, one of the railheads and all I could see in front of me was a snow-capped mountain. It filled my whole view. I remember looking at the snow and thinking how could that be, when it was so hot and I marvelled at how the snow glowed green in the moonlight. The gusting snow high on the mountain peak looked like clouds in the otherwise clear sky. I would have given anything for a few minutes up there in the cool air, out of the oppressive heat. When we moved around India, we took everything with us. From the train it was all packed onto horse drawn carts and mules. We carried our own kit. We didn't arrive at ready-made camps; we had to put the tents up when we got there after perhaps a twenty-mile march with a full pack in the stifling heat. You couldn't stop to rest and you only drank water when you were told to. On a long haul we would stop periodically at a pre-arranged place that was used regularly for camps. Here, there would be some masonry built Dutch ovens where the cooks would set up and provide our meals. It used to amaze me how we found these places. They were in the middle of nowhere, but the officers seemed to know what they were doing. After setting up camp and completing what duties we had to, we were allowed to fall out and the blokes would get on with their hobbies or play cards. We would be given some beer and it would usually end up with a singsong before retiring to bed to get some rest before an early rise and perhaps another long march.

The plains became really hot in the summer months and disease flourished. You didn't report sick unless it was serious. If you did you had to collect your kit and take it with you, so usually, we all mucked in, fetching and carrying for anyone that was ill, until they got better. Depending on what you'd caught, friends built a shelter in some quiet spot so you could rest, bringing food, water and what medicine was available until you were fit enough to return to your unit. At the height of the summer the sun parched the plains with virtually every blade of grass killed off and the soil dry and sandy, like a desert. Sometimes when we marched tremendous dust storms filled the hot air making it difficult to breathe. We covered our faces and marched on. When the weather and disease became unbearable the army would send us up to a hill station where it was a lot cooler. We had to march there though, uphill all the way. As we went up the mountains the air got thinner which made some of the men ill. The cooler climate was a welcome change to me, but it became cold at night. Our ailments from the plains such as prickly heat and other skin complaints seemed to vanish. Rich, green pine forests replaced the dry, barren, sandy plains and healthy, well-fed wildlife made a refreshing change to the scrawny animals down below. The monkeys were fun at first but soon became a nuisance, continually scrounging and nicking our food. After a short rest to recharge our batteries we went back down onto the plains and the heat. Of course the dry heat was not the only problem. After the summer came the monsoon when it rained continuously for weeks. If the sun did come out you became soaked with sweat only to be drenched again later.

The War started in 1914. By 1915 we were sent back to England before going to the front. We went home by ship and I for one was sorry to go. I had been there for four years and was used to the open spaces and lifestyle. We arrived back in England on February 1st, 1915. Soon after I got home I heard that my mother had died and I was given forty-eight hours leave to visit the family. When I returned from leave we were put on a ship to Turkey. We thought we would be going to France. The Turks had sided with the Germans and the powers that be decided to open another front in the east. We hardly had a chance to acclimatise to the British weather and we were back on board heading for the sun again. We reassembled at Avonmouth on 22nd March. It was a lovely morning in the bright, warm sunlight. Everyone was cheerful, joking with each other, but the embarkation was a right cock-up. Our Regiment was split up with us all being spread out on four different ships. We eventually arrived at Valetta, in Malta on the last day of March. The French sailors and their bands sang us in to 'God save the King' and 'Tipperary'. After coaling we sailed on, arriving at Alexandria, Egypt on 1st April 1915, Easter Sunday. Well, I'd never seen anything like it. The harbour was so packed we had to stay out at sea for three days before they could find room for us at the quayside. It was April 6th before we could disembark. Then, we passed through Alexandria to camp on the seashore by Mustapha Pasha. We re-embarked onto the SS 'Aragon' and set sail on the 11th April and two days later reached the Greek Island of Lemnos, off the coast of Turkey. We were to land on the Gallipoli peninsular by the Dardanelles, a tidal strip of water separating the peninsular from the mainland, leading to the Sea of Marmaria. Lemnos had a large bay suitable for the ships and was to be the rear base for the invasion. I was one of thirty five thousand British troops sent to take the peninsular along with seventeen thousand Anzacs, a mixture of Australian and New Zealand soldiers. The Turks had eighty-four thousand troops to defend it. The British main force was to attack at five beaches – S, V, W, X and Y. We were part of the 29th Division and our initial objective was to land by Cape Helles and form a line across the peninsula, including the height of Achi Baba, about five miles from the Cape. The Anzacs landed further up the peninsula.

It was 25 April 1915. I'd turned twenty-four earlier in the month. This was it, my first real action. The sea was calm, like glass. The blokes didn't say much as our ship made its way towards the landing area. The officers barked out orders and advice but I can't remember what they said, my mind was elsewhere. The British warships put up a tremendous barrage, shelling the coastline for hours in an attempt to make our landing easier. They couldn't go in too close; the Turks had laid mines to stop them. We climbed down rickety timber ladders onto the boats to be taken to the beaches. There was a hell of a commotion. The boats had suffered damage from the enemy fire and the seawater in them had mixed with the blood of those that had been killed or wounded previously and washed over our boots as we packed ourselves in. Everything seemed to be happening all at once and the noise was horrendous. Little steamboats pulled our string of boats towards the coast. We were supposed to go to V Beach but they said it was a death trap, so we were diverted to W Beach. About fifty yards from shore, they cut us loose and the sailors rowed us in with their backs to the action, but we could see what was going on. The Lancashire Fusiliers had gone before us and copped a right battering with over five hundred killed. However, a number had landed safely and established themselves on the beach. They won six VC's before breakfast that day. Some of our men were sick with nerves as we got closer and the sea was red with the blood of dead and wounded men. There were bodies everywhere Some were upside down in the water the weight of their packs pulling them down after they'd been hit. Bullets where whizzing past us, shells were bursting in the water and air above. Shrapnel was flying all over the place. Some of the guys in the boats got hit, including the sailors. One suddenly slumped over his oar. He couldn't have been more than a kid of fifteen. But we all were kids really. An officer shouted an order and he was moved aside. Someone else took over. It must have been awful for those lads, having to row all the way back and then bringing another boat full of troops knowing what they were in for. As we got closer to the beach

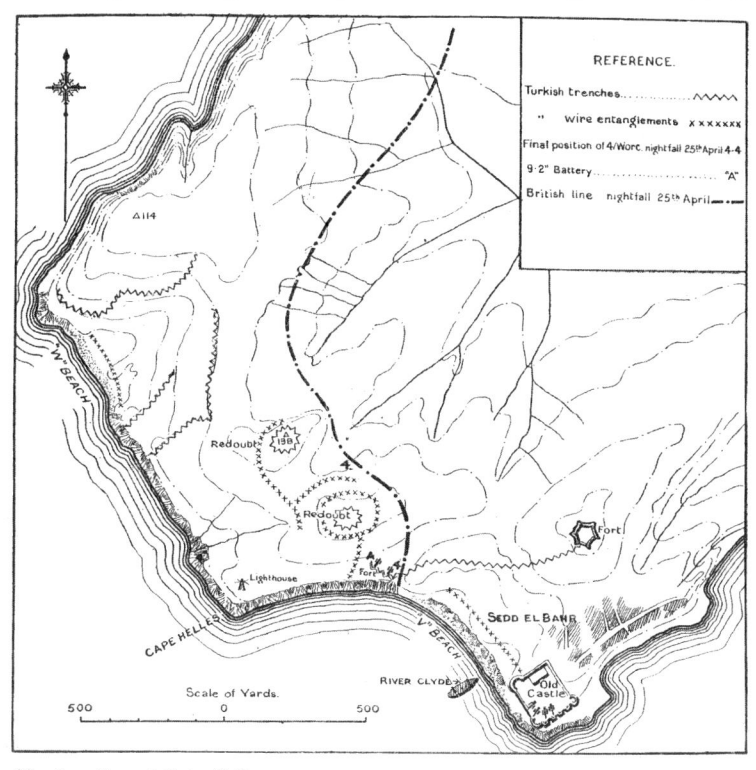

The Landing at Cape Helles

the worse it got. The shells from the Turkish guns were peppering the water all around us. Barbed wire was laid out in the shallows together with mines and they took a few boats out. Some blokes were sent over the side to cut a path through the wire so we could get closer in. Eventually we got close enough to get out and stand in the water to make our way to the beach. Men were falling all around as we went forward past the floating bodies. We all carried our packs and; I had to carry part of my Vickers machine gun. Another chap had the tripod. As we reached the beach bullets zipped into the water around us and I noticed the red sea foam breaking on the shoreline.

W Beach was a narrow strip of deep powdery sand in the shape of a crescent. It was about three hundred and fifty yards long and ranged from fifteen to forty yards wide. At either end the ground rose to high, crumbling cliffs. But in the centre the rise was more gradual and the defenders had elaborate barbed wire defences. Although the ships shelled the Turks there were plenty of them crowded in the trenches above us preventing us going forward. Their machine guns caused havoc and our men were running in all directions to find cover. Shell after shell burst in the air, sand and sea and splinters of shrapnel saturated the atmosphere. Land mines were concealed in the soft sand underfoot. Men were dropping like flies. It was carnage; dead and wounded all over the place. The stretcher-bearers were the real heroes. They didn't stop treating the wounded the whole time, despite being continuously under fire. We couldn't go back. There was only the sea. Some troops didn't get artillery support and were stuck on the beach in the open with no shade from the hot sun. Things got so bad that everything had to be landed at night, even the water and food. The men in charge of the packhorses and mules had a right game keeping them calm. We still wore our thick, coarse uniforms. It was very uncomfortable in that heat. It got cold at night and the thick uniform was most welcome then. We managed to find a track through the craggy, crumbling rocks and made our way up. We were on all fours at times, carrying our packs and equipment. We approached a narrow section of the cliff track and a young officer, one of the Lancashires, was clinging to the cliff face preventing me getting by. I asked permission to pass but he didn't reply and just stared at me. It was only then that I noticed he was stone dead; frozen in position, clinging to the cliff. We moved him out the way and continued. Eventually we reached the top of the cliff. We passed a large Turkish gun that had been blown off its mountings by the shells from our ships. Nearby was a dead Turkish officer. I checked him out but all he had was a full pouch of tobacco. I took that although it wasn't as good as ours, but I would smoke it later, sharing some with the others. We moved forward towards our first objective, 'Hill 138', dug in and established our position. Fortunately the chap carrying the tripod was okay and the 'Vickers' operational. The ammunition arrived too. We were ready for action. The enemy position was protected by a high, thick barbed wire entanglement and was virtually untouched by the ships barrages. There wasn't any way round so it had to be cut by hand. Volunteers came forward and all you could see was an arm raised out in the long grass, as a soldier would lie on his back cutting a path through the wire under a hail of enemy bullets. Suddenly the arm would drop and other volunteers would go forward until the path through was completed. Eventually enough paths were cleared and the position rushed and taken. We advanced and captured the next enemy position before dark and settled down for the evening. It was cold and rained that night. We were very anxious, lying in the open and exhausted from the day's battle. Many of our mates had been killed and we were running short of ammunition. We were expecting a counter attack during the night, but it didn't come, so we snatched what rest we could amidst the constant noise of action all around. The next day we moved on to help clear the Turks from their trenches above V Beach after which, we spent the rest of the day being reorganised, preparing for the next push forward.

4th Battalion digging in after the attack on May 6th

'W' Beach

During the coming week we advanced inland, digging in where we went or taking over old enemy positions. The terrain was mostly scrub and long grass. There were areas of cultivation and some lovely wild flowers. Now and then we passed dead Turks. We had to bury them and generally did this after dark. When night fell there was no moon, it was pitch black and silent. Everybody talked in whispers and listened for the enemy who were expected to attack. We heard some noises in front of us on one occasion, but couldn't see anything. I set up the Vickers aiming just below waist height and fired, gently tapping the side of the gun to pan the whole area and ensure nothing was missed. Immediately screams and moans came from the wounded enemy but I continued. I had to, it was us or them. If they had got through we would have had it. At first light it was a dreadful sight. The ground was littered with loads of dead and wounded Turks. I had cut them to ribbons with the Vickers. Many had limbs missing or hanging off and those left alive were screaming and moaning with the pain. I know they were the enemy but we couldn't leave them like that, so some of us went into no-mans land and gave them some water and bandaged their wounds as best we could. This was far better than the Turks treated our chaps. They were more likely to torture them and nail them to wooden crosses. From then on if it was dark and we heard the slightest noise, I would send a burst of machine fire just in case. I may have used up plenty of ammunition but several times I got the enemy and saved our skins.

Turkish Landscape - View from Hill 141

After a battle we would often let the enemy clear their dead. It would save us the trouble. At night we would bury our dead, including any Turks; it was hard work in that ground. They used to burn theirs. There were plenty of other things to do, such as collecting rifles and ammunition and any other litter of the battlefield. Nothing was wasted. During May we had a respite and for three days remained in reserve, away from the front line. We made the most of it, swimming in the sea and messing about, doing anything to take our mind off the situation. Our break ended too quickly and we pushed forward and set up again. My job was to give indirect and covering fire for the advancing troops. We picked a high spot and got ready. To our surprise we could see the enemy trenches. Not only that, we could see into them as well so they had no cover. These trenches were not in the front line, but feeder trenches where the reserves assembled prior to moving forward into action. Well, they were sitting ducks and I let them have it. They fell like ninepins as I panned their trenches and they had no idea where the bullets were coming from. They kept their heads down and poked their rifles over the parapet of the trench and fired into mid air. I kept firing until there was no more movement in the trench. I must have killed dozens of the poor sods.

On another occasion I was giving covering fire to an infantry attack by some Gurkhas on a Turkish position. They caught a hell of a pounding from the heavy Turkish fire with many killed and wounded. As the injured Gurkhas tried to crawl back through no-mans land to our lines, the Turks threw oil bombs. We couldn't go and help them. We could only watch in horror, leaving them to burn to a painful death.

Now and then we would be held in reserve giving us a chance to rest. We needed it. We had lost a lot of men including officers. Our advance slowed in the following weeks as the Turks resisted. I continued with my job, manning the Vickers, giving covering fire to our attacking infantry, constantly under fire as the machine gun was a prime target for the enemy. A bullet hit the Vickers causing the water-cooling jacket to leak. This didn't worry me. I was used to bullets and shrapnel whizzing close by. I calmly plugged the leak and continued firing. Suddenly, I felt a blow across my throat. It was as if someone had hit me with a sledgehammer. I was thrown right back across the machine gun nest. I must have been in shock, but I remember blood was spurting from my throat and I couldn't breathe. I was choking on my own blood. It was then that I realised I had been shot and tried to call out, but no sound came. It all seemed to take an age, but it was only seconds. Everything seemed in slow motion. I couldn't hear anything. I felt as if I was on the outside looking in. Then all of a sudden everything came back to life as shells went off around and the noise of the battle continued. My mates shouted and grabbed me dragging me clear and started to roughly bandage me up. I still couldn't breathe properly. The sniper's bullet had severed my windpipe, smashing through my adams-apple and damaging my vocal cords. I put my fingers into the wound to pick out the smashed bone and cartilage, freeing my windpipe to enable me to breathe again. It wasn't entirely successful, but at least I was getting some air into my lungs. They left me out of harms way and went back to their posts. I was now alone and could either stay where I was and perhaps die or be killed or try to get back to the first aid dressing station for treatment. I managed to get up and started to make my way back. I was in a dreadful state, still picking bits of tissue out of my wound and struggling for breath and the Turks were shelling the whole area. When I reached the dressing station it was pandemonium. They could hardly cope with the amount of casualties and the Turks shells were falling all around us. I couldn't do much about it so sat down with the others and waited to be seen. The shells were getting closer and some of the wounded men were getting hit again. The ground where I was sitting became wet and saturated my clothes. I thought a shell must have caught one of the water containers. But when I looked down I was sitting in a large pool of blood. The wounded chap next to me had been killed, some shrapnel had ripped his body open and his blood and blood from those next to him flooded the surrounding area. I felt that this was too close for comfort and decided to try to move to a dressing station further back from the front line. It was getting cooler and I had lost a lot of blood and was feeling cold. I took a thick greatcoat off a dead Turk. It was unused and neatly folded, but I had to be careful that I was not mistaken for the enemy. When I arrived at the dressing station it was quieter but I was a lot weaker and needed treatment very quickly. I heard that one of the officers was going round shooting the severely wounded men to save them any further discomfort. Mercy killing they called it. Well I wasn't going to hang about to be shot by one of my own. Not after what I had been through, so I decided to make my way back to the beach to see if I could get any help there. I can't remember too much about how I made it to the beach; my next memory was of being on board the 'River Clyde'. This was one of the ships that carried the troops in. It wasn't out in the bay though. They nicknamed it the 'New Horse of Troy'. It had been run aground by its crew to get the troops safely onto V Beach, avoiding the underwater defences and guns that they would have encountered in the rowing boats. It was now being used as a hospital ship and I was on the operating table. The medics were trying to fit different sizes and types of tube to join my windpipe back together. They didn't give me any anaesthetic; I had to be awake so they could know if it worked. I'm sure they must have given me something but I was in agony. In the event the operation worked and I could breathe reasonably normally, but then there was the wound to deal with. They couldn't do much with that and just cleaned and tidied it up, leaving a gaping hole. They said it would eventually close and heal with time.

V Beach with 'River Clyde'

That was the end of the war for me. I was sent back to Alexandria in Egypt for convalescence. While I was there we had a local Arab barber sent to cut our hair and shave us. Whilst tending me, he was fascinated by my bandaged neck and asked to look at my wound. I gently teased the bandage so he could view the damage. He jumped back in horror when he saw the gaping wound. It worried me how it might look when it healed. It did heal up okay in the end and I got my voice back albeit very gravelly. I used to wear a scarf at first to hide the scar, but over the years it faded and so I didn't bother. I returned home to England and spent the rest of the war testing guns.

Shortly after I got back I met Ivy. We married in 1917 and had two boys. After the war I was discharged with a War Pension of one pound per week. That wouldn't be enough, not with a family. But I had no trade. The army was my job. It was all I knew. Fortunately Ivy's family were in the building trade and gave me a start, first as a labourer, then as a stonewall builder. The money they paid me was all right, but the work wasn't that regular and we couldn't survive on my war pension. Ivy was resourceful. She opened shops selling second hand furniture, paintings and bric-a-brac. I helped with the deliveries. We made ends meet. In the mid thirties she rented a large house and took in lodgers. Over a period of time we took over several more houses. This worked well with her business sense and me collecting the rent, doing odd jobs and repairs. We made a great team.

In 1939 the Second World War started. After a time, my eldest son Eddie was called up but was discharged because of asthma. My other son Raymond joined up of his own free will. I went mad especially after what I had been through. Although I wasn't happy about it I supported him, tried to give him some advice. He survived and served with some distinction. They're married now and have their own children. They come to visit now and then and I tell the grandkids my stories. I wonder what they'll make of it all when they're older?

ROYAL ARTILLERY - Gunner Simeon John Hinton Morse

I was called up in May 1939, the month after my seventeenth birthday. I belonged to the T.A. (the Territorial Army). We trained every weekend at Witney Barracks and went for two weeks training at Chichester. When we got back, the Sergeant Major announced that it wouldn't be long before he had us b.....s back for good and it wasn't. I was posted to the Ox and Bucks. It was the first regular job I had had. I left school at fourteen and there weren't jobs about in those days. I picked up work wherever I could, did a bit here and a bit there, mostly farmwork. I was kept back when the rest of the lads went to France because I was too young. You had to be eighteen and three months to serve abroad in the army. There were twenty six of us that were too young to go. We were transferred to the 5th Battalion of the Light Infantry at Witney. We were on guard duty, mostly on airfields, Brize Norton, Rissington and Upper Heyford. Then we were sent to the Isle of Wight and we were on duty at the submarine base at Cowes. Then we were sent to the other end of the island to guard a top security station at Ventnor. This turned out to be a radar station, something that nobody knew about in those days. Security was tight. We were on duty at nights and it was freezing cold. It was the winter of 1940 and the wind blew as if it had come straight from Siberia and it snowed. We were knee deep in snow. One night I saw movement in a dark corner and ordered, "Who goes there?" and nearly bayoneted my own officer. In March 1940, I was transferred to the artillery and sent to Spitalgate near Grantham to train on twin L.G.s (Lewis Guns). From there I was sent to guard different locations, R.A.F. stations at first, Cranwell, Digby, Cottesmore, and Spitalgate. I met the girl who was to become my wife there. She was working on the base. Then I was put on the defence of Grantham. Marcos. the ammunition factory was there and that was a target for German bombers. We fired Bofors there. I was on duty at Gorse Lane. There was a searchlight party further along and they caught a Junkers 88 in their beam but we were not allowed to fire at it in case it fell on to the town. Then I was sent to Peterborough. We were back to Lewis Guns there. They asked for volunteers to return to Grantham and I volunteered straight away to get closer to my girl. I was on D site that time beside the canal.

    That was when I was sent to Blandford to make up the battery strength. I was given a week's embarkation leave. We set sail for the Middle East from Liverpool on The Strathmore. We were on the ship for six weeks. We crossed the Atlantic before sailing to Freetown, Capetown and Aden. I had never been abroad before, never been far from Oxford and I found everything fascinating. We weren't allowed ashore at Freetown but as soon as we docked, the ship was surrounded by natives swimming and diving for coins that we threw into the water. Some of the men wrapped their coins in silver paper before they threw them so that the swimmers thought they would find silver. We were at Capetown for three days. I went ashore the first evening we were there but on the second day, I was detailed to police duty, accompanying one of the South African policemen. I had never seen anything like it. We took up a position near a club. There was a sailor on the pavement and he was trying to fight everyone and everything. He was covered in blood and didn't seem to know where he was. "We'll have the Black Maria for this one," the policeman said. No sooner had we got him stowed away, than a soldier took his place. And so it went on until I returned to the ship. I had the third day ashore and, as we went out of the dock gates, we were met by a chauffeur driven car and six of us were taken out to a grape farm and entertained for the day. Everything was so cheap in Capetown. One of the soldiers came on board with a sandbag full of oranges which he had bought for one shilling. We couldn't buy oranges for love nor money back in England.

We called in at Aden. Then we went through the Red Sea and disembarked at Port Tufit. We went by train to Quassassin where they were establishing the new 8th army. The men were lined up in a square and an officer stood in the middle and spoke to them all but I missed it. I had gone down with sandfly fever.

I was now put on a Bofors gun detachment. There are fifteen men in a detachment, one in charge, 2 and 3 man the predictor, 4 fires the gun, 5 and 6 are ammo (ammunition) men , 7 lays the line, 8 lay for elevation. The rest are relief.

We travelled into the desert by train and disembarked at the railhead. All the supplies came to the railhead and were unloaded by the service corps. That was our first job, to defend the railhead. Then we took over our transport, a 3 ton truck and a Bofors truck. Our first duty was to guard the advanced airfields. The first one we reached was just a strip in the soil. There was nothing there. Then the planes came in, Kittihawks, and they had sharks heads painted on them. They really looked something coming in to land. The Germans used to come in on bombing raids and, at night, we would take hurricane lamps out and set them in line out in the desert, marking out false flare paths well away from the airstrip, so that their bombs wouldn't do any harm.

I didn't like the desert, it was dusty and dirty. The wind would get up and you could see these sand storms coming, kamseens they called them. Sand would get everywhere, in your ears and eyes and mouth, in the clothes and food and drink. We would drain our tea through a sieve and there would be half a cupful of sand in the bottom. The sandstorms would blow all day and there was no way you could get away from them. We guarded Wellingtons at one airfield and Marylands at another. They were flown by South African pilots. We were at one air strip where they were flying Bostons. They took off in threes, and those that were in the air circled until the whole squadron was airborne. They were taking off when those of us on the ground saw two black dots coming out of the sun, two Meschersmitts swooped down and shot one of our planes down. We opened fire straight away. We saw one of the German fighters going over the horizon with smoke pouring out of its tail and we heard later that it had crashed.

We were often strafed. George Everett had a hole shot through his bivouac. It had missed him by inches and we couldn't fire at the Jerry plane because our breech block had jammed. We met up with other troops from time to time and we came across some of the Gloucester Hussars. They had come out from England with us on the Strathmore. They drove General Grant tanks. One of them had been a man we all knew as Ginger and he'd been a real character, a right comedian. We all felt sad when we were told that he had been blown up with his tank.

We were detached to Tobruk and took up our gun position on top of an escarpment. The allies were preparing for The Push. The Jerries were piling in everything they had and the smoke and the noise, gunfire and planes flying overhead were a constant background. The Germans shelled Tobruk for two solid weeks before it fell. We were detached from it all. We were looking down on the scene and one of the men said, "They're fleeing for their lives down there." We were moved round the hill to the coast side to defend the shipping. The field telephone went. The bombardier answered it and he went beserk. His nerve gave way and he was shouting gibberish. It wasn't the first time I'd seen a man's nerves give way under the strain. "Here, give it to me," I said and I took the phone from him. We were ordered to blow up the gun and make our own way back. We didn't blow our gun up. We took the breech block out and dumped it in the sea. That made it completely useless. Then we started to move but I was the last to leave. The troop officer had tried to set his truck alight and he'd burnt himself quite badly. We had some ointment back in the gun emplacement to deal with accidents like that and I told them to wait while I went back and fetched it. When I returned, they'd all gone. There was no-one there at all. It was so still and so quiet. I didn't know what to do. I started making my way round the coast and I came to this beautiful bay with golden sand. It looked so peaceful but I knew it had been mined. It was marked with a skull and crossbones. I knew I had to move. I swam across and stumbled up the beach on the other side. There were all kinds of dugouts and caves dug out of the cliffs and there were still half eaten meals lying about. The men must have left in a hurry. I still had the world to myself and started up the cliff. That was when I saw two German soldiers waiting there. There was nothing I could do. I surrendered to them. They took me back to a building where I was shut in with a few more British soldiers. The next morning we were taken by lorry to the prisoner compound. I could hardly believe it. It looked as though the whole British army was there. They said 25,000 British troops were captured at Tobruk. Well, I was one of them.

Thirst was the main problem. It was torture. We were desperate for something to drink. We were there overnight, then, in the morning, the German lorries lined up, each one towing a trailer. We filed out and climbed into them, fifty in a lorry, fifty in a trailer. We finished up at Benghazi and were handed over to the Italians. It was terrible, terrible. We were put into these compounds and given a little drop of water each day and a hard biscuit. They were often mouldy. We also had a small tin of meat each day, although you couldn't identify it as meat. It was so hot in the sun that it came out of the tin like a lumpy liquid. We ate it though. There was nothing else and we were starving. Within days dysentery was rife. Men were desperate for food and were bartering with the guards for bread and water with anything they had, watches, rings, anything. It was hot and dry and windy and the wind blew the sand into our faces. The first water they brought to us was in petrol cans that hadn't been washed out properly. It tasted horrible but we were so desperate with thirst that we would have drunk anything. I can't remember how long we stayed in that compound but we quickly learned our first Italian word, Tamani (tomorrow). All our questions were answered with the word.

Then we boarded a ship, The Monviso. It had an Italian crew but a German gun crew. We were herded down into the hold, through a hatch in the deck and down a ladder. It was dark and dismal but I was so hungry, I could only think of food and I began to feel on the floor to see if there was any spilled cargo. And I found some dried apricots. At the most there were ten but it was the first food I had eaten in over a week other than the dried biscuits.

We were at sea for three days. We knew the allies were bombing ships and we worried that we would be bombed or torpedoed. We wouldn't have had a chance to escape, not through that small hatch. We came into the bay at Brindisi and were taken ashore by lighters. We were taken to an orchard for the night. It was too cold to sleep. We huddled together for warmth. It was a good job I was only dozing because I felt someone pulling my legs. One of the Italian guards was trying to steal my boots.

It was a relief to get into trains. We went to Camp 75 at Bari. This was like a transit camp. We had all our hair shaved off and we registered with the Red Cross there. Then we were transferred to Camp 54 at Farra Sabena, near Rome. There were 2,000 of us there. Most of the men were South Africans and a South African sergeant was in charge. He used to strut around the camp like a little Hitler. Eight of the men were black South Africans and the white Africans wouldn't mix with them. They absolutely refused to have them in their tents. They wouldn't listen to reason so we had them in with us. They weren't any different to us except for the colour of their skin. We were all fighting for the same cause but the whites wouldn't think that way. I must say that the

Once Upon a Wartime X

Italian guards treated the black prisoners exactly the same as us. We slept under canvas, 60 men to a tent. We had double bunks and two blankets each and we needed them. It was bitter cold at nights and it didn't help being so hungry. We had ersatz coffee in the morning. The only thing you could say about that was that it was warm. Our daily ration was a bowl of soup, a bread bun and a small piece of cheese, about an ounce, three times a week. There was water but it wasn't long before we became weak and dehydrated. Then one day tomato puree was added to our soup and it must have been bad. Virtually the whole camp went down with dysentery. That wasn't all. We started to itch. You first noticed men scratching under their arms, then other parts of their bodies- lice, body lice. We were infested with them. They brought in fumigators to deal with them. We could put our clothes in them. They killed the lice alright but the heat encouraged the eggs to hatch. We would put on the fumigated clothes and within minutes would watch the newly hatched lice crawling up our legs. I became so weak that I started having dizzy attacks and had to steady myself when I stood up and I was having trouble with my sight. My eyes wouldn't focus. I would see six or seven trip wires round the perimeter fence instead of one.

They asked for volunteers to work and I was one of the first to do so, anything to get out of the camp. Two hundred of us were detailed to unload coal and take it to a factory making steel. We were housed in a barn with triple bunks. I was in a state by this time. Boils were breaking out on my arms and legs and spreading all over my body. It was about this time that the first Red Cross parcels arrived. I never had one to myself. We generally shared them one between two or three. They contained tins of meat and cheese, jam and fruit, some tea and cigarettes. They were life savers. Some of the men ate the contents quickly but I rationed mine out carefully. The Italian people were kind on the whole and those that were working in the steel factory started bringing us in bits of food. I began to pick up a bit healthwise.

I palled up with Doug Bolton from the Coldstream Guards. He had been captured at the Knightsbridge Box at Tobruk. He wore a cap with the word Oxford on it, so we got to talking. He was concerned because when he got back from the work party, he found that his mate had taken some of his precious food. I told him I wouldn't play tricks like that so the two of us became best mates. He was a great mate. He stood by me when I needed help.

We were nearer the Swiss borders and two of the men escaped. They nearly made it to Switzerland but they were caught and brought back.

Then we were sent to Bergami, Camp 62. It was a wicked camp. There were all nationalities there, Slavs, Poles, all sorts. The guards were Fascists and they used to get excited. Doug and I volunteered for a work party and we were sent to work on farms. There were fifty in our party, 18 South Africans and 32 Brits. They asked if any of us had experience with saddlery. Doug and I had a quick discussion and I volunteered. I didn't know anything about saddlery but the saddler taught me all I needed to know. Doug worked on a farm. This made things easier for us because we could generally manage to collect something to eat, a few tomatoes or a potato or two. We would share whatever we had found when we got back to the camp. I began to get better and, now that we were a little stronger, we stopped being infested with body lice.

Then Italy capitulated. The Italian guards were getting excited. They didn't know what to do. At eleven o'clock they walked away. At one minute past eleven, we followed them. We all wanted to get back to our own sides before the Germans picked us up and sent us to P.O.W. camps in Germany. By two o'clock, we were in civilian clothes.

Those Italian women were heroes, so were the ordinary working men. They weren't interested in the war. They had had enough of it. We started walking through the countryside, making our way from farm to farm. We had to be careful. Italy in the north was still occupied by the Germans and there were plenty of Italian fascists who were prepared to give us away, especially as the Nazis offered a reward for each one of us that was recaptured. But a lot of the Italians were more than simply non obstructive, they were helpful and kind. We were careful not to abuse this kindness and only stayed at a farm for one or two nights before moving on. We wondered if the families who gave us food and offered us shelter were genuine or keeping us there until they could report us and get the reward. It must have been tempting because they were mostly peasants. We were doubtful of one farmer and we slept with the beasts that night rather than in the shed he had suggested and we left early the next morning. Sometimes the farmers would tell us to stay outside, well away from their farm, and then they would send us food. It was nearly always soup and bread. They also ate a lot of maize. They made a kind of porage from that which they called palenta.

We didn't seem to be getting any nearer Switzerland, so Doug and I decided to join the rebels in the mountains. We knew who they were because they rode bikes and had white handkerchiefs wrapped round their left hands. We met up with them in Gambia. We were given bikes and rode through to Brechia. We rode some way behind the man leading us but kept him in view. There were Fascists and Germans everywhere and we felt uneasy. We expected a hand on our shoulder at any minute. We went into a cafe and wheeled our bikes through to the rear and left them there. Then we came out of the front door, one at a time, and started walking towards the mountains. It was a steep climb. Doug and I found it tough going. It was 2,219 metres to their hideout. The rebels lived in a mountain shack and they were so disorganised that we decided to leave them after a few days. The only food they had was chestnuts which they cooked and we soon got fed up with the sight of them. They didn't have any blankets or any means of keeping warm and it was cold at that height, bitter cold at nights. We made our way back down the mountain and we picked up an

Irishman on the way. He asked if he could join us. We weren't keen. Three men were more obvious than two but we agreed to let him come. We walked through the city and spent the night at Leno. We washed and shaved as best we could in a dyke and started off the next morning, walking in single file with a fair gap between each of us. It happened that it was one of their religious festivals, the day of the dead, and crowds of people were assembled around the cemetery. We reached a T junction and Doug turned left but I missed him and carried straight on. Paddy, who was some way behind, followed me. People started looking at me suspiciously and I was getting worried. Then I saw some German motor cyclists approaching so I dived into a ditch and stayed there until well after the crowds had gone. A labourer came along and asked if I was English. He was helpful and told me which road I would have to take to catch up with Doug and we did find each other. I had followed the labourer's directions and, when I reached the town, I had stopped at a house and asked for food. An elderly lady lived there on her own and she really looked after me. I slept in a proper bed and had wonderful food. A neighbour had killed a pig and all their friends were welcomed to the meal they had, including me. We had pork, of course, and pasta. They also ate small birds about the size of sparrows which they wrapped in another kind of meat. They made enquiries to find out where Doug was and three days later we met up on the outskirts of the town. We never knew what happened to Paddy. We never saw him again.

We were in Gambara now and started moving from farm to farm again. One evening, we ate in the farm with the family, then the farmer took us out to a barn where we could stop for the night. We had to climb a ladder to get to the top of the hay. It was completely dark and we had to feel our way. As I stepped off the ladder, my foot slipped into a hole in the rick and I fell. I landed on the ground and I lay there. I couldn't move. I can remember thinking that I'd had it. They got me to the top of the rick somehow or other but I wasn't any better the next day. I lay there for five days. I had no movement in my arms and legs. I couldn't stay there and I knew Doug must keep moving. I tried to persuade him to go but he wouldn't leave me. The farmer brought a doctor and it was arranged to move me to an empty cottage down a track. I was there for eighteen days. I began to move my arms and legs but I still couldn't walk. It eventually turned out that I had fractured my pelvis. The doctor came and saw me and said that if I wanted to walk again I would have to give myself up so that I could get proper medical treatment. The next morning they brought a pony and trap and eased me into it. I was driven to Assolo and left on the bridge over the river. It was early in the morning and I was soon discovered by a man going to work. The police were fetched and they frisked me, then a car took me to hospital. I was the only Englishman there but I was beginning to cope with the language by then. I had a guard round my bed all the time I was there. I couldn't have run away if I had wanted. I was in traction, trussed up like a turkey with my leg tied to a rail and weighted down by a small sandbag. The Sisters of Mercy were wonderful and so were the local people. I had so many visitors that they had to be limited. An Italian soldier in the bed opposite me was having similar trouble. I used to watch his wife and daughter coming to visit him. He went home and I was told that he had died. That did upset me.

I was at the hospital for forty days, then I was taken by staff car to Mantova Hospital. I was on crutches by this time. There were all sorts there, English, Americans, all wounded. There was a lad from Birmingham who had shrapnel in his throat. I thought I saw a familiar shape and he turned round. It was Georgie Everett from our old camp. They were being moved by train when it was bombed and that was how he had been injured.

We were loaded into a hospital train and taken to Germany. I was graded for light work and was sent to a shoe factory in Dresden, working a stapling machine to make children's sandals but I couldn't cope with the standing. I was regraded and sent to a factory in Sudetenland putting glass fibres into mattress like parcels. We got up at 5.30. and worked in the factory from 6 in the morning until 6 at night. It was all forced labour in the factory. There were all nationalities there. One day, the sun shone through the windows and I saw all the glass fibres in the air reflected in the sun's rays. I was breathing that in and that wasn't my idea of staying healthy, so I reported sick. I then worked at the camp, in charge of two huts. There were 144 prisoners to each hut. One day 1,500 prisoners came in. They had been force marched from Poland and they were in a dreadful state. Some of them were near collapse. They told me that if any of the men had been unable to keep up they had been shot.

Food had been getting short for some time. We didn't have enough for these extra mouths but at midnight that night, three wagonloads of Red Cross parcels came in. The Germans wanted to put them on one side until the morning but we wouldn't hear of it. I can't describe what those parcels meant.

We could hear gunfire in the distance and it was getting closer. Then we got up one morning and the guards had gone. The gates were open and the boys started joining the columns of refugees and we went with them. We walked and walked and walked. We seemed to be walking for ever. We came to a level crossing and had to wait for a train to go through. There was a German officer there with eighteen horse drawn wagons of wounded soldiers from the Russian front and they stank. It was almost unbearable to be near them.

I asked the man on the crossing where the Americans were and he said they had reached Karlsbad, so my pal and I made our way there. The town is in a hollow and, as we went down the slope, we were accosted by a man waving a revolver. He was as drunk as a Lord and I thought, "Don't say we've come all this way and we're going to be shot by a drunk." We managed to work our way round him and reach the hotel in the centre of the town. We went in and told the American soldier that we were English prisoners. "Go upstairs boys," he said, "and find yourself a bed. Breakfast is at eight o'clock."

The next morning, we came down the curving stairs and smelt eggs and bacon. I hadn't seen eggs and bacon since I'd left home. I couldn't eat it though. I made sure I nibbled a bit but we had been so long without solid food, our stomachs couldn't take it.

The two of us walked back to No Mans land. I guess we felt a bit lost. A German staff car came along and we stopped it. We had the German officer and his chauffeur out and sent them on their way but I've still got the officer's cap and arm band and binoculars. Then we looked at each other and I said, "Can you drive because I can't"

Some more Brits came along and they piled into the car. We had one sitting on the bonnet and one on the boot and we set off. It was easy. We'd got it into our minds that we were going to Strasbourg. When we reached a road block, the Yanks would say, "O.K. Boys, straight through." We would stop at their depots for petrol and K rations. Then we were stopped by the American Infantry. "We can't have you boys driving round like this," the officer said. "You've got to go home," and they confiscated the car.

We were taken to a camp, issued with K rations and the next morning we were taken to Brussels in a Dakota. Everything was organised there. We were fumigated and documented and then out to the flight line. Dakotas were lined up there like you see cars on a motorway and we filed out to them, 27 to a plane We came into an airfield near Horsham but the pilot veered round so that we came over the white cliffs of Dover and we were home.

I had six weeks home leave and then I had another four but I was back to Grantham at the first opportunity. My girl had a special licence and we were married at Ropsley on June 16th. 1945. We had the reception in the school and somehow my mother in law had got hold of a leg of ham. I had to go back to the army until my demob number came up - 29. It took me five years to settle down. I had two daughters by then and I had to sort myself out. I got a job, coach building. I remembered how hard things had been before the war and I was pleased to get a job of any sort, but it only paid four pounds a week and that wasn't enough to bring up a family. So I went and worked for Fosters as a painter and decorator and I stayed there for thirty years. My leg's played up but I'm better off than a lot of the other lads and I get excellent care at the hospital in Nottingham but I've never forgotten how the nuns looked after me in Italy. I sent them some money as a thankyou. It took me a long time to save it but I wanted them to have it so that they knew I had never forgotten.

Once Upon a Wartime X

One of the Italians who sheltered
Mr Morse

Wedding Day

Mr Morse

MAILLY LE CAMP, BERLIN AND ALL - Jack Sparks

I went into the rag trade when I left school. I always liked people and I liked talking so it seemed like a good career. I worked for The Fifty Shilling Tailors in the High Street but when the war broke out, that was the end of my career. Clothes rationing had come in and there weren't the clothes to sell. I went and worked for the R.A.F. as a civilian in the 14th M.U. (Maintenance Unit) at Carlisle as a junior storeman. I was 17. As soon as I turned 18 I volunteered for aircrew. I reported to Padgate in March and I passed my medical and all the tests they gave me. It wasn't until I was preparing to be sworn in that they realised I worked for the Maintenance Unit. I was in a reserved occupation so I was sent back to Carlisle. I tried all kinds of ways to get them to release me so that I could join the R.A.F. but without success. I made a thorough nuisance of myself, like clocking in at half past ten in the morning but my boss would look over his glasses at me and say "You won't get released by playing up like that so give up trying."

But I was determined to join up so I made up my mind to go and see Mr Moon. Mr Moon, C.B.E. was the civilian head of 14 M.U. Getting to see Mr Moon was as difficult as landing on the moon but I was determined. I walked across the site to the main building. No-one stopped me. I found his office and knocked on the door. I was just about to go in when a secretary dashed up and tried to keep me back but Mr Moon called out and told me to go in. I told him that I wanted to be released so that I could join the R.A.F. He called his secretary in straight away and told her to type up my release papers and take them in to him for signing.

Well, November the 25th was a bad day for the German Reich. Hitler got the flu and I joined the R.A.F. although I began to wonder why I had bothered in those first weeks. We went to Blackpool for initial training and we were there for seventeen weeks. There were three hundred recruits lined up the first day when the Flight Sergeant appeared. He was the smartest man I had ever seen. He shone. He had his pace stick under his arm. He stood there and surveyed us and a hush fell over the waiting recruits.

"What a shower," he said and there was an expression in his voice that made us feel small.

Then he introduced himself. "I'm known as Bill the Bastard and you'll soon know the reason why."

We did.

He demanded the highest standard in everything.

We were issued with kit. We received inoculations for every imaginable disease and a few that hadn't been invented. We received instructions and directions until we didn't know if we were coming or going. Then we were marched down to the barbers to have our hair cut - shaved was a better description. None of our hats fitted after that.

I'm six foot two, so I was always the marker when we had to fall in and we spent the best part of the day marching from one place to another. It was three days before Christmas when we fell in and marched through the town. As we passed a departmental store, I glanced in the shop window. Immediately there was the order bawled out so that the whole town could hear, "Squad halt." We stood there listening to the sergeants footsteps advancing down the column of men. Then he was standing immediately behind me, breathing down my neck.

"Do you like looking in shop windows, sonny?" he demanded.

I mumbled a reply.

" Flight, left turn," he commanded and immediately all the men turned to face the window.

"Go and have a look then sonny," he ordered.

I told him it didn't matter but he had given an order and I had to go and stare in that window for several minutes before I was allowed back in line and we continued the exercise. I never let my attention wander again.

Some of the men found it hard to take the discipline but, at the end of our training, we would accept an order without question. Later on, it was that very discipline that probably saved our lives. Some of the men were homesick. Homesickness is a funny thing. You can be as brave and as tough as the next man but you can be homesick. One of the men in our group was homesick. He was an only child and he'd never left home before but we kept an eye on him and, by the time we left Blackpool, he was one of the lads, the same as everyone else.

I went for training to the Wireless School at Yatesbury and then went on to Whitchurch for gunnery training which I completed as a Sergeant Wireless Operator Air Gunner. All aircrew were at least sergeants.

Then I went to my first posting at Whitchurch in Shropshire. I settled in then went down to the pub for a drink. There was one other airman at the bar and we spent the evening together and walked back to camp. That was one of the most fortunate experiences of my life. We assembled in a hangar the next morning. I think we all felt a bit lost. Then the pilots were instructed to make up their own crews and my drinking partner of the night before pushed his way through the crowd and asked me to join his crew. Flight Sergeant Fred Browning was older than most of the other pilots. He was 33. He was totally unselfish and always had the welfare of his crew at heart. I asked him once if he never wanted to fly low. He replied that it was something every pilot would like to do but he had a crew on board and they were his responsibility. Their safety was the most important aspect of his job so while they were on board he flew high. That was typical of the man. Fred was the pilot. I was the wireless operator and Ron Walker the navigator. Norman Barker was the bomb aimer, Arthur Richardson the Flight Engineer, Ken Smart the mid upper gunner and Bob Thomas our rear gunner. We made thirty sorties together. They were more than just mates. They were family.

One night, coming out of Berlin, we were attacked by German fighters. We were thrown to the floor and the Lancaster was riddled with bullets. It's funny how one reacts in such a situation but I found myself lying on the floor singing, "Oh God Our Help in Ages Past", at the top of my voice. Then a miracle happened. The shooting stopped and the plane was droning steadily on through the night. Bullets had gone through the radio and it was useless. So too was the communication system. There was no way we could know what had happened to the rest of the crew. I had to check on them. I clipped on a portable oxygen bottle and went to find out. Each of these bottles lasted ten minutes so there wasn't time to hang around. The rear gunner was dead. He had been shot to pieces, He couldn't have known what had hit him. His turret was in a hell of a mess. I thought the mid upper gunner had suffered the same fate. His feet were dangling loosely in the air but, when I contacted him, he gave me the thumbs up sign. He was O.K. The bar on which he rested his feet had been shot completely away but there wasn't a scratch on him. The others were carrying on with their jobs. They may have been shaken but they didn't show it. It was in situations like this that the importance of the discipline and training we had received came to the fore. To a certain extent, the crew reflected the attitude of the captain. He was quite calm and was concentrating on getting the plane back to England. He needed terrific strength to hold the stick down and had to force it down with his knees to keep it in position.

I clipped on fresh oxygen bottles to work on the wiring and managed to repair the intercom. We could at least talk to each other and that helped a lot. We weren't so isolated. But there was no communication at all between us and the ground. The communication system was not the only thing that had suffered in the attack. The plane was riddled with holes and there was a hole, five feet in diameter in one of the wings exposing the petrol tank. It was a wonder it hadn't exploded. We didn't have time to think about it. The priority was to get home and that wasn't going to be easy. The weather was terrible. We had been told before we set off that we were to expect winds of forty miles and hour. In fact we flew out with a tail wind of 130 m.p.h. This meant we were flying home with headwinds of 130 m.p.h. The wind was so strong that several planes were blown off course. We were. The navigator had a hard job keeping us on course. We flew on steadily, a lone Lancaster in a dark sky, our speed drastically reduced. There were 73 aircraft missing that night.

We came in over the south coast. Visibility was O.K. but it was still night. All the aerodrome lights were out. There was an air raid in progress over London and all the lights had been switched off so that the Germans could not identify our air bases. We had no way of communicating with the ground. We started to circle, hoping that the sound of our engines would attract attention and they must have done because there was the pundit, the flashing beam sending the two letters DF in morse code - Dunsfold. That was where we had to land. The lights were out there as well when we got there. Before we had set out for Berlin, I had collected about three dozen red Verey cartridges and put them in the plane. The others had teased me about it, wanting to know if I was planning a firework display over Berlin but they came in useful that night. I fired off about fifteen of the cartridges and suddenly the lights were switched on and we were going in to land. We knew it was going to be tricky. There was no means of lowering the undercarriage and we couldn't be sure that the Lancaster would hold up. We were all in crash positions, sitting with our backs to the mainspar, all except the captain of course, waiting for the crash. Everything happened so quickly. We didn't have time to think. There was a Flying Fortress lying on the runway that had crash landed three days before. All we had time to notice was the name Passionate Witch and the brightly coloured illustration painted in the way that the Yanks decorated their planes. Suddenly the Lancaster was skidding down the runway and the captain was fighting like mad to keep it steady. He was landing at 140 m.p.h. and he didn't have any brakes or any means to slow it down. Then the Lanc slewed round and ran into the Passionate Witch. What the Germans had started, we finished off for them. It was at that moment that the petrol tank burst and there's nothing like the smell of petrol to make a crew move. It was seventeen feet to the ground but we didn't think about it twice. We jumped through the escape hatch and I jolted my back as I landed. I didn't realise how badly I had hurt my spine but it was the injury that was to eventually invalid me out of the R.A.F. But I had my life. Bob had been killed but the rest of us were lucky and we were lucky yet again because the petrol didn't ignite and we were able to walk away.

We had a new plane and a new rear gunner, Bert Buckman. We didn't expect any trouble when we set out to bomb Mailly le Camp in Northern France. It was May 1944 and this was one of the raids in the run up to D day, not that we knew anything about that at the time. Major supply routes, military concentrations, anything that could have helped the enemy to repel the invasion when it took place was being bombed to destruction. Mailly le Camp was a military barracks situated on the edge of the village of Mailly. It had been French but then it was occupied by German troops and it was believed that a Panzer division was billeted there. It would be a 'milk run' we were told.

We took off from Elsham Wolds and it was a night like any other. We were getting used to them. We zoned in to Mailly without any trouble. The pathfinders had been in and the flares had been dropped but instead of being called in, we began to circle waiting for instructions. We had maintained radio silence as usual on the way in but when we switched to the frequency to receive our instructions, we got the American Forces' news broadcast and a lot of other garbled messages. Churchill insisted that French lives and property must be protected so the leaders were taking extreme care. They now think the radio problems were caused by the Germans jamming them. We began to circle fifteen miles from the target, waiting to be called in. The sky seemed to be full of Lancasters circling and there was a danger that we would touch or be touched by another of our own planes flying above or beneath us. There was one we missed by the skin of our teeth.

"I don't like the look of this," the captain said and he flew thirty miles out from the target and started circling again.

We were called in to bomb at 12.32 hours. We should have bombed at 12.15. Those seventeen minutes had given the Germans time to muster their forces and there were four night fighter stations within reach. Their fighters were waiting for us when we returned. So were their searchlights and their anti aircraft guns. The losses were dreadful. We lost 42 planes that night, the highest percentage of losses in any raid up to that point. I saw two Lancasters going down, screaming towards the ground with a trail of smoke behind them.

Until then, a raid over France had counted as a third of a mission. We had to make three French runs to equal one over Germany but after Mailly le Camp that was changed. Raids over France counted as a full operation.

We had completed thirty operations and now we were sent to different stations as instructors. We had lived and flown together as a crew and become close and important to each other, Now we simply said 'Goodbye' and went our own way.

I didn't fly any more operations but I still flew from time to time. There was one time when a pilot asked me if I would like a flight, so we set off, just the three of us, the pilot, the navigator and me. We'd just taken off when he asked us if we minded if he flew a bit low. It seemed he had a girlfriend near Lincoln and he wanted to impress her. Well, we hadn't realised exactly how low he meant. He missed the trees but only just. At one point we looked up and saw a bus travelling along a road above us and a line of white faces staring out of the windows. We found the house alright and circled it several times. The girlfriend was obviously expecting us because she came out and waved. On the way home, we saw some Italian P.O.W.s loading a hay cart. "Let's have some fun with these," the pilot said and he started to bomb them - in a Lancaster. The Italians ran in all directions.

We weren't exactly popular when we got back especially as the plane we had 'borrowed' was the one the CO liked to fly.

My back became very painful and I had to have an operation on my spine. I was invalided out in 1947 and I returned to my old job. It was a strange feeling being back in Civvy Street, having to think for myself about ordinary things like what to eat and what to wear but it was deeper than that. We had been living for a day for all those years. Now we had to make a life for ourselves. We had to live for the future.

Fred Browning, Norman Barker, Ronald Walker and Arthur Richardson were all awarded the DFC following the air raid on Berlin. Jack Spark received the DFM and was commissioned on December 13th 1944.

December 1941

Jack Spark, 103 Sqdn Elsham Wolds February 1944

Blackpool 1941, Jack is 5th from left standing

Once Upon a Wartime X

(l to r) DFM, 1939/45 Star, Aircrew Europe with France and Germany Clasp, Defence Medal, Victory Medal

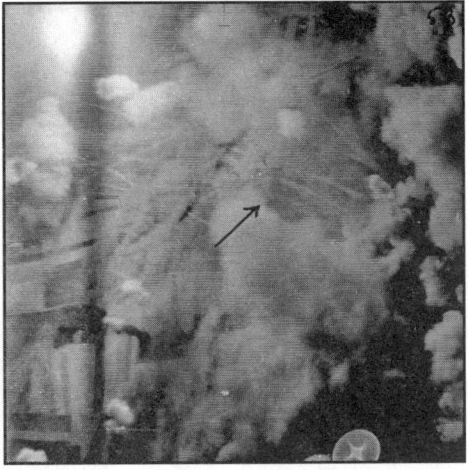

Taken by the Bomb Aimer, Norman Barker at 8,000 ft

(l to r) Arthur Richardson (Flt. Engineer) and Fred Brownings (Pilot)

FIRE FIGHTER - Reg Seward

I was working in a tobacconist and sweet shop when I was called up and I volunteered for the fire service. I don't know why. It was just something that took my fancy. I was a trainee fire fighter until the end of 1943 when I was sent to Sutton, near Hull, to the Central Fire School. It was an intensive course and followed all aspects of fire fighting but the accent was on aircraft fires.

To be honest, I hadn't really known what to expect when I volunteered but I soon found out when I took up my first posting at R.A.F. Blyton. This was a heavy conversion unit which meant that pilots were converting from two engined planes to four engined such as the Lancaster. There were a lot of crashes, 6 or 7 a day and most were fatal and that was the loss of seven men in each crew. Our job was to save as many lives as possible but we would be beaten back by the heat and flames. One member of each crew of four was trained to wear a full asbestos suit and attempt to rescue the airmen. The only type of suit available then meant that you could only be in it for ten minutes, fifteen at the most because the only air available was inside the suit. We would get as near the plane as possible before putting on the hood and the crew would keep a fine spray of water on us the whole time but it was often a desperate attempt in desperate conditions.

Fire crews faced terrific dangers especially when attending a crash. We only wore leather jerkins over our uniforms and the fires were so intense that bullets would fire from the gun turrets. There were belts of ammunition going off but we were generally far enough away for it to feel like a light punch. You got used to it but it was alarming at first especially to the trainees.

One of the greatest dangers was when a plane crashed with a bomb still fast in the bomb bay. The flames and heat could set it off at any time which could and did kill the attending fire crew. I thought the threat from oxygen bottles were worse. There would be a nest of these, generally under the cockpit area. I would have to stand on these to rescue an airman while another member tried to cool them down with a spray of water and all the time, I knew those bottles could blow up and me with them but my only thought was to get the lads out as quickly as possible.

We were called out one day to a plane that had crashed into a wide dyke at Laughton. It had been raining heavily so the ground was like a bog. What we hadn't realised was that what we thought were puddles of rain water were in fact mainly puddles of petrol from the plane. We were wearing issue flying boots made of suede. I took the hose reel down the bank to lay foam on the area but, as I got down there, the ground ignited and my boots were in flames.

Luckily for me George Gibbs, a gentle giant of a man who was one of the fire fighters, saw what was happening lifted me bodily out of the boots, carried me up the bank and set me down on the fire tender. I was nearly a lot hotter than I had bargained for.

We had to attend a crashed plane that had landed in a wood. It had gone right down one of the rides and the plane was in pieces, so were the crew. They all had to be accounted for and we collected the pieces of the men and put them in body bags. It had to be done. I can't say that we ever got hardened to some of the things we had to do but we became used to them. On this occasion, we had a trainee with us. By the time we finished, we were cold and wet and hungry. There was always a hot meal waiting for us when we got back and this time, it was sausage and chips. We tucked in, so did the trainee, then he couldn't face any more and he ran outside and was sick. It had really got to him.

Fire tenders always had to be present on an airfield. Our duties were divided into three days. We were on duty twenty four hours at a time. The first day was duty on the fire tender on the field, the second was our rest day, the third was on the section, checking hydrants and maintaining equipment. We still had time for relaxation. I met the girl who was to become my wife at Blyton, Madge Croft. She was a W.A.A.F. telephonist

My second posting was to Elsham Wolds. Madge was posted to Group one Headquarters at Bawtry at the same time.

There were two squadrons of Lancasters at Elsham. When there was a raid on, a plane took off every thirty seconds and, of course, a fire tender had to be in attendance and we were still there when they returned. That was a tense time. I suppose we all counted them back but you couldn't allow yourself to think of those who hadn't returned. You had a job to do and you had to get on with it. I can remember them coming back from the raid on Mailly le Camp. We lost a lot of planes on that. We were kept busy because a number of planes were damaged,. There's one Canadian Air crew Navigator who still reminds me at reunions of the time we chased the Lancaster he was in down the runway in the fire tender because their brakes had failed completely. They pulled up O.K. but the crew must have set a record for the speed with which they exited.

Elsham Wolds was different to Blyton. It was a fully operational station and the crews were experienced. We were still kept busy. One plane made a forced landing and ran into a tree and all on board were killed except for the rear gunner. The whole of the turret had broken off and landed some way away from the plane. The gunner suffered a broken leg and a few bruises.

Another time we went out to a plane that had made a crash landing. It didn't seem too bad when we got there but when we got into it, we found every member of the crew at their positions and they were all dead. There was not an injury on them. They had been killed by the blast.

We practised dropping sacks from the Lancs rather than bombs. The crews flew practice runs along the Humber. They were preparing for Operation Manna, taking food to the Dutch who were starving.

The war was drawing to a close and we began to ask each other, "What are we going to do when this is all over?"

It's difficult to describe the atmosphere on a station in the war. The thing that comes back to me over all the years is the comradeship, the feeling of togetherness. And then it was over. Madge and I were married but there was no chance to settle down. I was still in the R.A.F. and there was still plenty to be done. I was sent to Stanstead and then to India. I loved India Then I went to Japan and we were stationed near Hiroshima. The damage there was horrific but I didn't like Japan. You had to watch your backs there.

I was demobbed in 1947 and I went back to my own job and I've regretted it all my life. I should have stayed in the R.A.F. I felt fire fighting was as essential a part of the war as air crew. We were all part of a team and I missed it.

RAF Station Blyton, 1943 1662 Conversion Unit

Mr Seward

NAVY DAYS - Douglas Martin

I volunteered for the navy when I was seventeen. I would have preferred to go in the air force but there was a nine month waiting list for those wanting to train as rear gunners and I didn't want to wait that long. I was working in a grocer's shop in Boston. All my friends had joined up and I wanted a uniform too. I signed on at the recruiting centre in Lincoln in June 1942 and on August 31st., I reported to H.M.S. Royal Arthur, in other words, Butlins Holiday Camp. It had changed from Redcoats to Redcaps for the duration of the war and I joined 2,000 other would be sailors for basic training. There was a notice over the entrance which said, "Our true intention is all for your Delight." We experienced blistered feet, loss of teeth, shaven heads and puncture marks in assorted parts of our bodies where we had been vaccinated. Our W.R.E.N. cooks used the kitchens that had, in peacetime, been used to provide meals for the holidaymakers. I noticed they had a white powder which they stirred into our food and, when I asked, they told me it was bromide which was to be added to control our sex drive!

I was then posted to H.M.S. Valkyrie on the sea front at Douglas on the Isle of Man. That was where I heard Lord Hawhaw, the traitor who broadcast propaganda on German radio announce that the Germans had sunk H.M.S. Royal Arthur which was a bit of a miracle as it was a land station in the middle of Skegness. The hotels in Douglas, the Isle of Man, had been taken over for military use. The hotel next to us housed Italian internees but we didn't see them. I was training in R.D.F., Radio Direction Finding. There were plenty of characters in the navy and I met one of them there. My superior officer was Jon Pertwee. He would arrive on parade with his cap low down over his eyes similar to the way the guards wear theirs and a blue and white striped scarf wrapped round the lower part of his face. The navy is full of tradition and Jon Pertwee made sure that we didn't forget any of them even though we were on dry land. The W.R.E.N.s would drive the vehicles on to the parade ground and they would have to fasten them to the wire fence as if they were boats. He decided that the lanyards on our uniforms must not be more than seven inches long. He would stand at the gateway with a pair of scissors in his hand and if he thought our lanyards looked too long, he would cut them off.

In 1943, I was drafted to Portsmouth barracks for advanced radar training and then joined H.M.S. Allynback at Barry Docks in Cardiff. There was C and M (Care and Maintenance) staff on board when I arrived and they realised I'd never been on a ship before. I was fair game. I was sent to get two buckets of fog from the fog locker and told to look for a left handed hammer. But it was the

76

Once Upon a Wartime X

naval slang that threw me at first. They seemed to have their own language. The toilets were the heads and cocoa was ki.

The Allynback was a merchant ship that had been converted to a support vessel for beach landings. It fairly bristled with guns. I was a radar operator on searching for surface and aircraft approaches as well as manning the warning sets. Our first job was to provision the ship and it was all hands to assist. I was carrying a side of bacon up the gangway. I felt it start to slip and I couldn't hold it. Well the gangway was steep and the sides of the ship were high and the bacon was greasy and there was only the net to hold and then I lost it. I stood there and watched as it fell into the sea in the gap between the dock and the ship's side. Well I was put on a charge for that. I had loss of leave which meant I could not go ashore at the next port of call and that was Gibraltar. We'd set sail as soon as the ship was provisioned. We were in a convoy and we were making for the Mediterranean. I had never been abroad before. I'd hardly been out of Boston and that journey was a real eye opener to me and, when we docked at Gibraltar, I stood on the deck completely mesmerised by the scene in front of me. The main thing I remember now was how it was lit up. We were in the middle of the blackout at home and here, the whole place was lit up.

We were the first convoy to make it through the Mediterranean since Monty had taken over in the desert. We had been issued with white duck suits. They were made of calico and they were stiff. We had to soften them by washing them in salt water. We hugged the North African coast. We passed other British ships making for home loaded with prisoners on board. We could see the towns and the Arabs on the shore. We saw dust storms and German planes in plenty, dive bombing and strafing. We were on the constant lookout for U boats but we made it through to Alexandria. It was a different world. The night skies got to me, the brilliance of the stars and the huge moons. Then there were the smells and the noise and the atmosphere. It was marvellous.

Ships of all kinds were mustering in the harbour preparing for the invasion of Sicily but German divers got in amongst us and attached limpet mines to the ships. Two ships were blown up within five minutes of each other. We had to maintain a 24 hour patrol in motor boats. We dropped charges into the water that would stun the divers.

Operation Husky, our destination,. was Syracuse in Sicily and our mission was to escort six vessels to the beach area for invasion and to provide anti aircraft gun fire and other support in the landings. As we approached the island, a ship in the convoy astern of us was torpedoed. We didn't stop. There were others behind that would stop to pick up the survivors. Scores of aircraft were passing over our heads. The landings commenced at 3a.m. on July the 8th. The noise and the gunfire was terrific. Cruisers and Destroyers were bombarding Syracuse. We were attacked by Italian aircraft. The fighting was going on without let up. Then, on the 11th, we were hit by a bomb and two of

77

our crew were killed. Two of the Stukas were shot down and we didn't have any more dive bombing attacks after that. It was soon after that that a Spitfire was shot down and the pilot was rescued and brought on board. There was no let-up in the fighting and food was getting short on board. We were rationed to one slice of bread each a day. Another Spitfire was shot down into the sea and the pilot was rescued. We moved location then to Catania. Mount Etna was smoking and expelling a fine ash which seemed to cover everything and all the time there was the noise of gunfire. Now the allied airforce was in control. Four squadrons of Spitfires arrived from Malta and 12 squadrons of Kittihawks. We picked up two more pilots from the sea. We moved location to Cape Passero and then on to Port Augusta. We could see things going on ashore and I was amazed to see an L.N.E.R. locomotive travelling along the coastal line.

We located an Italian submarine and we forced it to the surface by dropping depth charges, then we sank it with shellfire. Then we upped anchor and made for Malta. We had to get the pilots back to their base. From there, we returned to Alexandria to prepare for the invasion of Italy. We picked up convoy additions at Tobruk, Tripoli and Malta. It was while we were at sea that we heard that the Italians had surrendered and the captain ordered that we should splice the mainbrace in celebration of an easy landing. Our rum ration was generally two to one, two parts of water to one of rum but when we splice the mainbrace, it was neat rum and Navy rum is strong stuff.

Salerno was the worst fighting experience of the war, far worse than D day even. Salerno is at the end of a bay with a steep, mountainous area on the left as we approached and marshy, flat area to the south. And the Germans were waiting for us. There was a Panzer division there and we knew it as we approached. It took five days to complete the landing at Salerno and, at one stage, the Allies almost withdrew. We hadn't expected the ferocity of the opposition. They had heavy guns built into the mountains and they were firing constantly. We held our position and kept up the fire. Shells were falling all around us. There was a tank in the marshes that was firing at us but the shells were either falling short or going way over our heads. Ten wounded soldiers from the Ox and Bucks were brought out to our ship and taken down to the sick bay. Then one of the shells hit us, an 88mm. It went right through the sick bay and those soldiers were killed. It was about mid-day. I didn't have a life belt so I went down to my locker to fetch it when there was this terrific explosion and an overpowering smell of cordite. Men were screaming and there was complete darkness. A group of men had been resting at the table behind me and they were all killed. One of them was my pal. I was thrown into the net where the hammocks were stored. I didn't know what to do . X and Y doors were closed and couldn't be opened. They were the bulkheads that kept the compartments watertight. We weren't sinking. There was nothing I could do so I stayed where I was. A hole had been blown in the side of the ship about seven foot wide and

Once Upon a Wartime X

the steel had been split open in the same way that you open a tin of sardines. I could look out of the hole and see the beaches and watch the battle in progress. We were under constant gunfire but the anchor was eventually lifted and we moved out but not before the Tiger tank in the marshes had been destroyed by a Dutch Monitor ship and a Lysander.

The next morning, we sailed out to the end of the bay to bury our dead. We had watched a hospital ship doing this each morning and now we joined her. Each body was sewn into a canvas sheet and weighted down with a shell. There was a service on board and then each body was committed to the sea. I had a lump in my throat as Bob Luffland, my pal, sank beneath the waves. After the burials, their belongings were auctioned amongst the crew and the money sent to their families. We were all subdued after that. There were three hundred of us in the crew but we were a tight knit group. We were like one big family and something like that affected us all. Then the Warspite was hit and nobody knew where the shell had come from but a Dornier 217 had been shot down and we picked up the crew. They were arrogant. They were only young men but they acted as if they were superior. They were taken for interrogation and it seemed that they had dropped radio controlled bombs and it was one of these that had hit the Warspite. We were ordered to take the Germans back to Malta for further questioning and then we were diverted to Bizerta where the ship was to be repaired. The crew were sent across the desert to Tunisia and we were billeted with French Tunisian families. That was an experience, being woken in the morning by the Muslim calls to prayer and the donkeys braying and seeing the sort of sights that I would never have dreamed about back in Boston. The family where I stayed had a radio and they listened to the B.B.C. Foreign Service on that. It seemed they had had Germans billeted on them earlier in the war and they had left the radio behind.

We returned to the Alynbank in October and set sail for England. The ship was to be decommissioned and was to be one of the ships that was to be used as a block ship for the Mulberry Harbour at Arromanches but we didn't know that then. We were trailed by a German plane as soon as we had passed Gibraltar and then the U boats attacked as we went through the Bay of Biscay. They were firing acoustic torpedoes at the rear of the ships. We gave them everything we had. It was a cat and mouse game and there was a tension on board but you pushed that tension to the back of your mind and got on with your own job. Some ships zig-zagged in an attempt to get away from the acoustic torpedoes that were chasing them but they didn't make it. We lost two ships that way. We were alert for U boats the whole time. Provisions on board were getting very low and we were living on hard biscuits and chocolate. Our captain was a man called Vivian Wyndham-Quinn and he was a real character. He was related to the Queen. He was 6 foot 7 inches tall and he would walk round the ship in his dressing gown. He had a chicken that accompanied him that was called Henrietta and he didn't like us having too much gunnery practice in case it upset her egg laying. He radioed ahead to Greenock and said that he wanted fish and ships for the whole ship's company on our arrival. As we anchored in the Clyde, two drifters came out from Greenock with the food. It was great, the best fish and chips I ever had.

My next ship was H.M.S. Serapis, a 2,000 ton destroyer based at Scapa Flow. It was one of the 23rd Destroyer flotilla on Russian Convoy duty. It was a bit different to duty in the Mediterranean. For a start, it was cold, so cold, that if a man fell into the sea, he was only able to survive for a matter of minutes. The ice settled on the deck and rigging and it had to be cut off to save the ship from becoming top heavy.

We escorted American ships to Murmansk, Liberty ships mostly. These were emergency wartime ships, put together quickly and they were flimsy. They didn't ride the waves, they drove through them. We would wait for them to arrive off Iceland. Then we would fall in alongside them and the convoy would set off for Murmansk. It wouldn't be long before we hit the pack ice and we would be forging through it from then on. It gave an eerie sound of crushing and moaning as we forced our way through it. We weren't allowed on deck because of the conditions and if we did have to venture out, we had to fasten ourselves to the rail by a rope so that we couldn't be washed overboard. We were well into the Arctic Circle and I really earned my blue nose certificate which we were awarded the first time we crossed it. Our quayside berth was at Polyano, a Russian town and it was a cold, miserable place. We were allowed ashore for two hours each afternoon but the Russian people weren't friendly towards us. They were suspicious because we weren't wearing uniforms but were wrapped up in thick duffle coats. Some of them really thought we were German spies. They were keen enough to barter with us. They wanted anything but mainly bread, razor blades, chocolate and cigarettes, but all they could offer in exchange was husky dogs and we wouldn't have been allowed to take them on board even if we wanted them. The Russian army guards, the oil tanker crews, the police and other workers were all women We spent most of our time in port chipping ice off the ship's structure to prevent it capsizing.

The German U boats used to lay in wait for us between Bear Island and Finland. One day, a ship in the convoy was hit by a torpedo. It didn't sink immediately but it was listing and we were detailed to pick up survivors and sink the ship so that it didn't cause an obstruction in the channel. The rest of the convoy steamed ahead while we went to the aid of the stricken ship. It was dark and snowing and very cold. I was on watch when the radar picked up an echo. I waited a few seconds to check it and make sure it wasn't a wave because heavy waves like we were experiencing that night could sound on the set, but the echo came again and it was steady. I reported it to the captain. It was identified as a U boat and within a few minutes it came to the surface to check the kill it had made. Their captain knew the convoy had steamed on and obviously hadn't realized we had stayed behind. Our captain manoeuvred the destroyer so that our guns had the U boat in sight and he ordered the guns to fire but the 4.5 guns were frozen solid and they couldn't be fired. But the smaller machine guns did. The U boat crash dived. Our captain ordered full speed ahead and prepare to ram the U boat but we passed right over it so we fired off depth charges to zero depth and blew it up. Then we returned to the sunken ship. It had almost sunk by this time and men had been thrown into the sea. We could see where they were because they had little red lights attached to their life jackets and they showed up in the dark. We threw rope netting over the sides and moved slowly amongst the men but none of them could catch hold of the ropes. Their fingers were too numb and cold. There were more U boats in the area and we were like a sitting duck. We didn't dare to hang about any longer and the captain gave the order to steam ahead and catch up with the convoy. I think we were all silent as we drew away from those red lights blinking in the darkness.

We had to go into Scapa Flow for repairs at Christmas and that was fortunate because our flotilla sailed on Boxing day to attack and sink the Scharnhorst. We saw them returning and they had been badly knocked about.

Then we were deployed to the south coast, off the Isle of Wight, to prepare for D day. We did countless runs along the north French coast, watching out for U boats. We challenged one boat and it gave the wrong signals so we blew it up and it was one of our own motor torpedo boats. We were allocated a beach section at Arromanches for D day. Can I ever forget? I can relive every second of that day. As the dawn broke, the sea was covered with ships, ships of all shapes and sizes and the soldiers were going in in those shallow landing craft. It was rough and it had been rough for the last few days and a lot of those men were sick, physically sick. And overhead the planes patterned the sky, all of them droning steadily towards France, towing gliders behind them. Then the heavier bombers followed them. Hitler didn't stand a chance. And the noise- it was the rocket ships mainly, the rockets shooting and screaming through the air and they never stopped and the shells from the heavy guns going over our heads with a particular sound as if they was sucking all the air along with them. The bombardment was indescribable. The Germans soon rallied but it was their metal stakes with mines attached positioned along the shoreline, just beneath sea level that did the damage. Two British ships manned by Norwegian crews were blown up within five minutes of each other by these. mines. We were positioned half a mile inshore from the Ramilles and the Warspite and they were bombarding Caen with half ton shells. It went on non stop.

We were detached the next day to escort H.M.S. Lord Roberts back to Portsmouth for damage repairs. She was a six inch gun monitor ship. We returned to Normandy but the war was moving on. We then went to Norway for the attack on the U boat pens. Our next duty was to escort The Queen Mary to America. Winston Churchill was travelling on it. We reached the Azores but we couldn't keep up with her. The Queen Mary was that fast. Only the cruisers could keep up with her. I was transferred to H.M.S. Zest. She was being commissioned and we went to the Mediterranean for sea trials. This was in August 1945 and it was great to be afloat without fearing U boat attacks. We were in Malta for Christmas and I met my brother there. I hadn't seen him for two and a half years. He was a telegraphist and the captain persuaded him to apply for a post on The Zest as our telegraphist had been taken to hospital with appendicitis. It was great to have him on board but it wouldn't have been allowed if we had still been at war. Blood relations weren't allowed to serve on the same ship.

We then visited Lisbon on a showing the flag exercise. It was great. We had a wonderful time there but the war was over and so were my navy days. I was paid off at Chatham and went home to Boston. I missed it all. I missed the excitement and the companionship and I missed my hammock. Hammocks are really comfortable once you get used to them. The silly thing was that I'd been given my hammock along with my demob suit and all that went with it but I couldn't be bothered to carry it home and I sold it to one of the spivs that was waiting at the dock gates.

I was 22. I had packed a lot into my life but the navy had given me confidence and a career. I didn't go back to the grocer's shop, I joined the G.P.O. and settled back near the place where I was born.

Once Upon a Wartime X

Proclamation

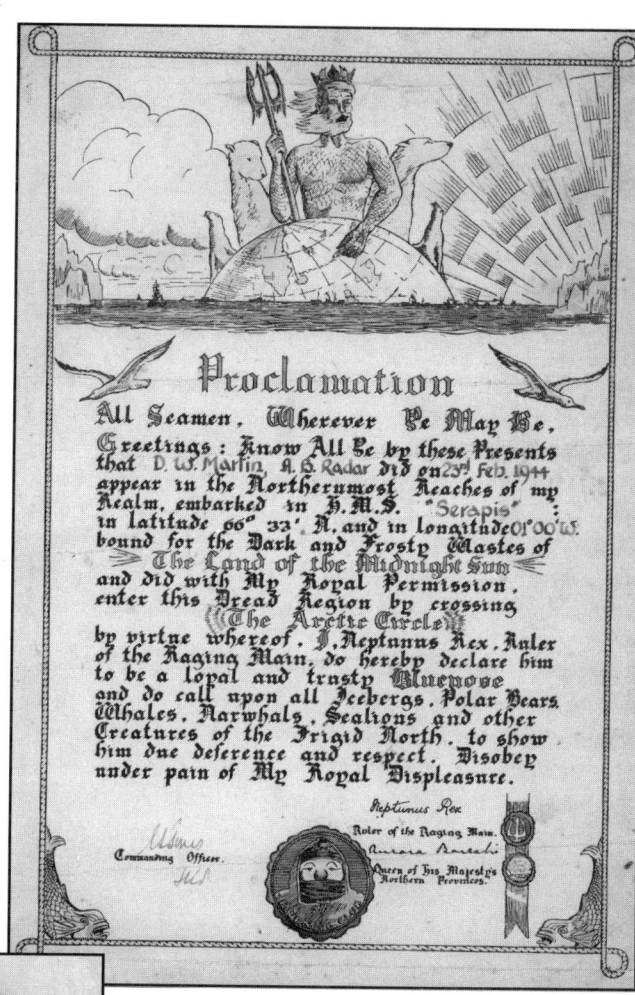

All Seamen, Wherever Ye May Be, Greetings: Know All Ye by these Presents that D. W. Martin, A. B. Radar did on 23rd Feb. 1944 appear in the Northernmost Reaches of my Realm, embarked in H.M.S. "Serapis": in latitude 66° 33′ N. and in longitude 01°00′W. bound for the Dark and Frosty Wastes of The Land of the Midnight Sun and did with My Royal Permission, enter this Dread Region by crossing The Arctic Circle by virtue whereof, I, Neptunus Rex, Ruler of the Raging Main, do hereby declare him to be a loyal and trusty Bluenose and do call upon all Icebergs, Polar Bears, Whales, Narwhals, Sealions and other Creatures of the Frigid North, to show him due deference and respect. Disobey under pain of My Royal Displeasure.

Neptunus Rex
Ruler of the Raging Main

Queen of His Majesty's Northern Provinces

Commanding Officer

Douglas Martin

THE POLISH SOLDIER - Jan Dutkiewicz

I was born in Saouk in Eastern Poland in 1912. I can remember the First World War. We had soldiers billeted on us and we had to live in the kitchen. I was one of five children. My mother died in 1918 and my father married again and had five more children. We were a big family. I got a job in a factory that made buses when I was thirteen but when the factory closed down, I lost my job and there weren't any more to be found. The Depression was as bad in Poland as anywhere else. I was a member of Marshal Piesodski's Army. That was similar to the Territorial Army in this country. I had passed as a cadet and that meant that I could delay starting my national service for three months but things were so grim in the depression that I pleaded with them to take me early because there was no work.

I worked as a medical orderly and, when I finished my time in the airforce, they found me a civilian job on aircraft maintenance in one of the hangars. I lived in lodgings and that took most of my wages but I had a job, a roof over my head and food to eat. Then on September the 1st, we were bombed by the German Luftwaffe. It was totally unexpected. There had been talk about the German threat but the bombing was a complete shock. I was in the hangar when the bomb hit us. Fortunately it was lunchtime and not many people were on the airfield. I had taken some papers to the office and was at the entrance when the world seemed to collapse around me. There was this sudden noise and the air was filled with dirt and dust and, as it settled, I could see the damage. Three of the men had been killed but one was still alive although he was badly injured. I managed to get him across to the van and drove him to the hospital but he died in the night.

We didn't know what was happening. There were rumours and counter rumours. We carried on repairing the aeroplanes. Then, on September the 17th, we were told that the Russians were coming. An officer came across to the hangar about eleven o'clock and told us to prepare ourselves. We were moving south. We went out to the main road and commandeered lorries that were passing. It was wartime and we were entitled to do that. We stopped a chocolate van and a few of us climbed into that. The driver wasn't keen on coming with us. His wife was pregnant and the baby was due any time. He wanted to get home but he didn't have the choice. He drove us down to the Roumanian border. When we reached the crossing point, we threw our rifles away, crossed ourselves and walked over into Roumania. We made our way to Bucharest but the capital was already packed with refugees so we were sent on to Tulda. We had plenty of money but it was Polish and we couldn't use it. Nobody wanted

Polish currency. We didn't have anything to eat. A Roumanian lady gave me a glass of milk and it was the first food I had had for several days. I went to a bank and changed my Polish money into Roumanian but they only gave me a fraction of its value. It was a peculiar time. We had no way of finding out what was going on in our own country or anywhere else. There were plenty of rumours. Men were worried about the families they had left behind in Poland and some of them did go back. The driver of the chocolate van stayed with us though. He had heard that the Russians had overrun our base. We also heard that the Polish army was reorganising so I sold my overcoat to pay for the fare and made my way back to Bucharest. I went straight to the Polish Embassy and volunteered for the Polish army in France. I was directed to another office and, as I left the Embassy, a man offered to show me the way but he took me in the wrong direction. He was asking me all kinds of questions and I began to get suspicious. I realised he was a spy. Roumania was full of German spies. I looked out for them after that.

I signed on for the army and was told that I would be travelling to France as a civilian. I was paid in Roumanian money and told to go to Duzau and wait there until I was called. Ten days later, I reported to Bucharest and boarded the train for France. We were on the train for four days, travelling through Yugoslavia and Italy. We had no food throughout the journey but we were buoyed up with the hope that we were going to be given the chance to fight for our own country. We left the train at Lyons and the French didn't welcome us. They didn't want us there. We were greeted with shouts and catcalls - "Go back home. - You've brought us into the war.- If it hadn't been for you, there wouldn't have been a war.........."

We stayed in France for a month. We were billeted in huts that had been in use in the First World War. We were near the Spanish border. There was plenty of food, mainly bread and soup but we were completely isolated from the local people. We were quite comfortable but we didn't know what was going on. Like the rest of the men in the camp. I wanted to get on with it. I wanted to get out there and fight the Germans.

We were told to always be ready to move out at a moment's notice but it was midnight when the call came to move, We marched through the night and reached the docks as dawn began to break. We were loaded on to ships and taken across the sea to Oram where we were billeted in stables. We were only there a few days when we were ordered to fall in and were marched down to the station. That was when we saw our own priest cycling down the middle of the road. He was wearing his soutan. He waved and called something out. It did our morale good to see someone from home.

We travelled in goods vans. There was plenty of water on board but no food. Every evening, the train would pull in at a station and food would be laid out on trestle tables for us. We finished up at Casablanca., not that we saw much of it because we were stationed on the outskirts. We weren't there long before we marched down to the docks and set sail for Liverpool. There were 21 ships in our convoy and we sailed right out into the Atlantic before we turned for England to avoid the German U boats. One day we had a German plane circling round us the whole time. We were told they were taking photographs but we felt uneasy while it was there. When we landed, we were taken straight to a hutted camp and put into quarantine. Some of the men were suffering from malaria.

Because I had been a medical orderly in Poland, I was sent to the Polish hospital as a sick bay attendant as soon as I had been cleared. I saw plenty of England in the next four years. I was a member of the Polish army and I always worked with Poles. In 1944, we went across to Normandy and went up through Belguim, France, Holland and Germany and we had plenty of injuries and sickness with which to deal. There wasn't time to stop and think. We were near Hanover when peace was declared. Some Polish women who had been in forced labour in Germany came to help with the patients and that was how I met my wife.

I am Polish too. We lived in the west of Poland where my family had a farm. I worked on the farm and so did my brother and sister. Things didn't change much when the Germans first overran the country but it wasn't long before things started to get difficult. They wanted us to go and work in Germany. My sister volunteered to go but I didn't, nor did any of my friends. Then the Germans started rounding up young people and taking them off. Some people started sleeping out in the fields or woods so that they wouldn't be caught. If they were found, they were shot. My father made a dugout under the ground and we slept down there but it wasn't very comfortable and I got tired of staying down there so I went and slept in my own bed and that was the night the Germans came into our house. They ordered me to get up. They gave me time to dress and pack a few things but they stood and watched me the whole time. I didn't have a chance to escape. Then I was taken to the station and sent by train to Hanover. When I got there, I was put in a room and told to wait. I didn't know what was going to happen to me. I waited there for three days. I didn't have anything to eat in that time. Then a man came by and gave me a piece of bread, but he was looking round and seemed frightened that someone had seen him. He told me not to tell anyone that he had given me bread because he would have been punished for doing it.

On the Monday morning, a German came and collected me and took me back to his farm, He gave me some soup and bread, then he took me out to the fields and gave me a basket with a strap that went round my neck and told me to plant the cabbages it contained. I threw the basket on to the ground and told him I was not going to carry it. It was far too heavy. I didn't mind planting the cabbages. I was used to doing that work on our own farm. He just shrugged and went away. He wasn't a bad man. It was his wife and son that made life difficult for me. There was myself and a Polish man who were used as slave labour. There was no rest, no relaxation but the worst thing was not knowing what was happening in the rest of the world or being able to contact our own families. We were fortunate that we had been sent to a farm and not a factory. Those people had a dreadful time. We did have food and shelter.

The farm was near Hanover which was heavily bombed. At first the bombers came at night. Then they started daylight raids and we would stand and watch them, silently urging them on. I saw Hanover burning. Sometimes bombs dropped in the fields but we carried on working, day in, day out, every daylight hour.

Then one day an American officer turned up in a jeep. We had no idea the allies were so near. He told us that all Polish nationals were to make their way to the camp at Reden. I can't explain my emotions as we made that walk. I didn't mind how long it took. The bad days were over. It was at the camp that I met other Poles and heard their stories and how they had been treated. I was much stronger than most of the other refugees and I went and helped in the sick bay and that was where we both met. We knew immediately that we wanted to be together and my husband was determined that we would be married before he returned to England but we wanted a proper Catholic wedding. Then we heard that the priest he had seen in North Africa was in Berlin and he phoned him and, after much persuasion, he agreed to marry us that next Saturday. There were hundreds of Poles waiting there when we married, all of them hoping that the priest would marry them. We were all married in batches of seven and, because we had made arrangements, we were married in the first batch. When we got back to Reden that evening, a tea had been laid out for us and one of the wards emptied so that we could have our first night on our own. Then my husband went back to England and I joined him in December, 1946. We had nothing. We set up home in an old Nissen hut. Our eldest son was born there and we were happy, happy to be together and to be free. We've worked hard and we've done well. Our sons have had a good education and this is our home. We own every stick in it. It's all ours. There were days in the war that we never thought we would be so lucky.

PRISONER OF WAR - Joe Cavanagh

I left school at fourteen but I was eighteen before I got a job. I tramped miles and miles looking for work but there simply wasn't any to be had, not between the wars in Manchester. I picked up a few odd jobs but nothing more than pocket money jobs. I was one of seven children, the second son. We were lucky that my father was in work. He worked for the council as a night watchman. We didn't starve but there was no spare money in our house and there weren't any luxuries but it didn't worry us. It was the same for all the families along our street.

We used to look after the children for one of the neighbours and when she came to collect them one day, I asked her if she would ask her husband if there were any jobs at the mill where he worked. She called in a couple of days later and said that her husband's boss wanted to see me the next morning. I was up at the paper mill early the next day. I saw the boss and started work straight away. I found out afterwards that I wasn't being paid the full rate for the job but I didn't complain. I was so pleased to find work and be able to take money home at the end of the week.

It was noisy working in the mill with all the machinery. Rolls of paper went right up to the rafters and then descended like huge paper chains. We felted heavy material like hessian for rooves. There were tanks of pitch and the machines took the paper through that. Other machines cut and trimmed and rolled. We were also making waxed paper in which bullets were wrapped. There was an increasing demand for that. My job was to keep the rollers soaped to stop the paper sticking.

My brother was in the Territorial Army and, after the war broke out, I decided to join as well. The very next day my call up papers came. I was posted to Gainsborough, to the Royal Artillery, the searchlight division. We did all our training there, then we were posted down to Aldershot where we did more training on rifles and machine guns. Then we were sent back to Gainsborough and were posted to the searchlight section. There were ten men in a section. 1, 2 and 3 were spotters. 4 was the man that turned the wheel to direct the light and number 5 was the electrician. 6 and 7 were the listeners. They had a piece of equipment like a big ear trumpet that could pick up approaching sounds. Then there was the corporal and the cook and a spare man that allowed us to have one day off in every ten. Number 4 had to manage the light. A searchlight is a big, heavy piece of machinery. They came in two sizes. The 90 cms and the 150 cms. The smaller one could be moved by a bar but the larger had to be directed by turning a wheel. He would turn this and point the beam upwards, following instructions from the other members of the team. I was number 5, the electrician. I had to change the carbon rods. I had to listen to the RT for instructions. There were two carbon rods which had to be changed regularly, one every three quarters of an hour and the other one every hour and a half but I would have to wait for instructions before I touched them. I had to fit in with the other searchlights in the line. Sometimes I would be told to wait for three or four minutes but we had to be careful. It was essential that the carbon did not burn too near the mirror that reflected the light because it would have blistered the glass.

We lived in wooden huts close to the light and there would be searchlights every quarter of a mile at different vantage points. We manned searchlights round Lincolnshire mainly. One site was where Salveson's is now and another time we were on the light behind the Ram Jam down the A1, but we couldn't take advantage of it because we were on duty twenty-four hours a day, manning the light throughout the night and cleaning and repairing during the day. We could be manning the light from dusk to dawn several nights running, then we would probably have a night when we weren't needed at all. One of us would have to stay on duty though in case we were wanted and had to wake the rest of the crew. There were some explosive reactions when that happened.

Some soldiers think we had a soft option but it was a responsible job. The Germans were carrying out heavy raids on the industrial midlands. They had to be stopped reaching their targets. If we could trap one of their bombers in our beams of light, then they were easier to shoot down. Once we had caught an enemy plane we would keep it in the beam. Then, when one of our fighters got it in their sights, they would signal to us by flashing their lights and we would switch the beam off so that we didn't blind them. We cheered like mad when they shot one of the Germans down. One searchlight crew did a stupid thing. They switched their beam off when the allied plane signalled to them, then they switched it on again and blinded our own men. The plane crashed and all on board were killed.

The most important thing was to identify the planes. I got good at identifying German planes. I did it by sound. Their engines missed out on every third beat. We weren't allowed to shoot unless we were given the order because there was the fear that we would shoot one of our own fighters down. Our own planes had their own code and they would flash different coloured lights to show us that they were friendly. The code was changed each day. The German pilots were cunning. They would find out what the colours of the day were and they would flash the same code so that we would think they were one of ours. Another trick they had was to fly amongst our planes so that it was difficult to pick them out. One German bomber actually landed on an airfield along with ours that were returning from a raid. The crew repaired their plane and took off again before the R.A.F. woke up to what was happening.

One of our first postings was to Colchester and it was the time that we were on the look out for parachutists. We were expecting a German invasion at any minute. When the soldier on guard failed to get an answer to his, "Who goes there?" he shot in that general direction and the rustling stopped. The next morning, the farmer came round and wanted to know who had shot his horse.

The Luftwaffe would drop bombs near us trying to put us out of action. One night, the searchlight unit alongside us received a direct hit. There was a terrific explosion. It was so close that we were completely deafened and didn't get our hearing back for days. There was only one survivor and he had been hiding behind the bar in the pub. He was so scared by the raid that was in progress that he wouldn't leave the place despite the fact that he was needed and they had sent a soldier to fetch him out. He was court martialled for cowardice.

We didn't only use the searchlights to catch enemy planes, we used them to guide our own, especially when they were coming back from a raid, swinging the beam from left to right. We would swing it towards the airfield that was their home. As the plane approached the airfield, we would swing the beam in a circle, three times in one direction then three times in the other. If a plane was damaged, we would be directed to guide it in to the nearest airfield. Aircrew often came round and thanked us for the help we had given them the next morning. They would invite us to go up for a flight with them. I never went but most of the other lads did.

Then I was sent to a camp. As I went to cross the parade ground, a sergeant asked me if I knew how to pack a bag. When I told him I did, he told me to pack mine and get down to the guard house. I was picked up by a lorry and taken to another camp and that was how I came to join the Durham Light Infantry, the 50th division. They were having their numbers made up ready to leave for France. We landed at Arromanches on the 10th of June. We went across in an American ship and they really looked after us. We'd taken our iron rations but we soon chucked those away and replaced them with American goods. They kept giving us cigarettes and chocolates. Well I emptied my bag except for absolute essentials and filled it with these goodies. I even stuffed my jacket with chocolate. It kept me going for a long time. We put our bags in the lorry and whenever it caught up with us, I replenished my stock.

We fought our way up through France and into Belgium. We saw the lights of Paris but we never went into the city. One day, my friend and I were sent to check out this French chateau. It was a beautiful house and the table was laid ready for a meal but there was no food, only a big jug and a lot of small bottles of water. I stuffed the small, bottles in my blouse and took a good drink from the jug. I didn't know what it was but it wasn't water. It burnt a hole right down to my stomach. Then I followed my mate. I took one step outside and that was the last I remembered. I had drunk neat Cognac. The rest of the lads enjoyed the bottles I had with me but when one of them asked me if I wanted a drink, I told him what he could do with it.

Then we were making our way forward to meet up with the troops that were landing in Arnhem. We had to fight our way along the road and we were sitting ducks. The road was on top of a dyke and the Germans were waiting for us on either side. Eleven of us were sent on reconnaissance one night. We were walking in single file when a voice shouted, "Achtung."

"What was that?" my pal asked.

"It means we need to move," I told him and we dived out of the light and into a ditch. There were five of us in our ditch and the others were on the other side of the track. Then the shooting started. There was a German sniper causing trouble and we got him in the end but we hadn't realised there was another one and he got the chap next to me, shot him through the mouth. We kept shooting until we had run out of ammunition. Then, all we could do was wait. A short while later I found myself staring at a pair of black boots. A German officer was towering above me. He spoke English. "Where are the rest of you?" he demanded. I told him there had only been eleven of us and he said that he could do with some soldiers like us in his own troops. We had kept his whole division at bay for twelve hours. Then he ordered me out of the trench. He wouldn't allow me to pick up my bag, instead he ordered, "Raus, raus." There was one man in the other ditch and he came across and joined us and the officer hurried us back towards his lines. There were wires on the ground and I tripped full length over one of them and, as I fell, the shooting started up. We were caught in the crossfire and the other allied soldier was killed. I wanted to go to him but the officer told me he was dead and hurried me on. A German soldier seized my watch and the officer was furious. He made him give it back to me but he needn't have bothered. Another one had taken it before we had gone a hundred yards. The officer took me to a holding pen where there were other allied soldiers. I was feeling bemused, hardly able to believe that this was happening. I told the soldier beside me how I felt, how I couldn't understand that I had been caught like that. We hadn't been aware that the Germans were so close.

"You can't understand," he returned. "I came out of my tent to go across to breakfast and there they were parachuting down and we were surrounded."

We were taken to a moated castle later on that day and the following morning, we were lined up and ordered to march. We marched all day and the following one and some of the men were having trouble to walk but that didn't bother our German guards. They were all riding in horse and carts. Then we reached the station and were loaded into cattle trucks. The minute the doors were shut on us, the sirens went and all the Germans disappeared and we were there like sitting ducks with the bombs falling round us. We were in those trucks for two days and two nights and it was dreadful. There was nothing to eat or drink. There was no sanitation, no room to lie down or sit in any comfort. We went across Germany in fits and starts often stopping for air raids. One of the men in our truck was in a dreadful state. He had malaria and was calling out for water. It was raining by this time and I put my handkerchief out of the slat until it was soaking wet and then I wiped the man's face with it and squeezed some of the moisture into his mouth.

We reached a station and were marched from there to the prison camp. There were three sections, French, Russian and British. The weather had turned wet and cold and I wasn't the only one to have inadequate clothing. I was in my shirt sleeves. It had been warm when I had been captured. I had twenty five cigarettes left and I traded them with a Russian for his big overcoat. Later on one of the French prisoners gave me one of their uniform blouses and I wore that a lot of the time, so much in fact that a lot of people thought I was French. The French were better off than we were from the start. They received Red Cross parcels and had enough to eat but I only received one in the whole year that I was a prisoner. One day, our guard said that the French were throwing away food and he took me with him to see. They had a container of soup that they didn't want so I took it through to our section. I went to fetch my billycan and when I returned it had all gone. I didn't even get a sniff of it. We were always hungry. You know those Swiss loaves, well we had one of those between ten of us each evening. We had a bowl of what they called soup when we got up in the mornings but it was little more than hot water. There was never any sustenance in it.

We had to work. My first job was at the crematorium. They brought the bodies in boxes. There wasn't time to make proper coffins. A lot of people were getting killed in the air raids. It got so bad at one time that we had to dig a hole and lay the bodies in a shallow grave. One of the German ladies pointed at one of the bodies and told me to cover it. I couldn't understand her language but I knew what she meant. She gave me a bit of tin to put over the man.

Then I was sent in a work party lifting potatoes. We managed to tuck a few in our blouses for our own use. Each hut had a stove in the centre of it and we were allowed ten blocks of fuel a day to heat it. Once we had got it warm, we would put the potatoes in the stove and bake them. One day, the guard pulled me aside and told me I was fatter than I had been when I went out in the morning and he poked me in the waist where the potatoes had settled. Then he looked at me and said, "Tomorrow, you bring me some," and I did.

I became quite friendly with that guard. He must have been seventy years of age and the German civilians were as hungry as we were. He let me know what was going on and he alerted me to the number of food parcels that the French were receiving. Then we were moved from the farm to work in the sand pit, loading sand into carts that ran along rails to tip into a big container. One day something went wrong with the machinery and immediately a cry of sabotage went up and the S.S. were called in to sort it out. They were dreadful men and the boy that was working with me was shaking with fright as they approached us. I told him to stand up to them. They were bullies and wouldn't react if they felt threatened. When the first one came up to me, I stared at him straight in the eye and he backed off but the lad flinched and shrunk back. Immediately the German lifted his gun and struck the lad in the mouth with the butt of his gun. The lad's face was bashed in and his teeth had been knocked out. He was in a dreadful state and had to be taken to hospital. Our elderly guard went to the S.S. man and spoke to him. That night he came over and said goodbye to me. He had been posted to the Russian front for daring to criticise a member of the S.S. "That's what I get for trying to stand up for you," he said sadly.

I gave him my address and told him to get in touch with me when the war was over but I never heard from him. He was an old man and conditions on the Russian front were dreadful.

The prison camp was a miserable place. We were always hungry and there was a lot of illness and depression. I was taken ill and the doctor was called in. He said I was to stay in my bunk and he told the German guards that I wasn't fit to work. There was the young man who hadn't recovered from his injuries in the hut as well. Then the S.S. guard came in and ordered us both out to work. I felt really ill but knew I had to move. I got to my feet and staggered out of the hut but the lad was too sick to move. The guard said they were taking him to hospital and they did take him off but we never knew what happened to him. He never came back.

We didn't know what was happening in the outside world. There were rumours of course but our lives seemed to go on in the same way. There were two things that changed. The guards became more relaxed and the allied bombing increased. There was a railway and a wood yard behind the camp. One night the Yanks were bombing the railway but they got the camp instead and the P.O.W.s that had been in one of the shelters were killed and so was one of the guards. He had been in a brick building at the woodyard. Two of us were sent to clear it up and look for his watch. He had possessed a watch that my mate envied. It was a big silver pocket watch with four little doors that opened. We searched through the rubble but we didn't find the watch and we went back to the camp. When we reached the hut, my mate said, "They won't find it either. I've got it here," and he tapped his pocket.

"You fool," I told him. "If they'd seen you, we would have both been shot," but nothing more was said about it.

It was only a couple of days after that, that I was wheeling a barrow towards the gate and one of the men told me that we wouldn't be there much longer, the Yanks were on their way. Then one of the German guards told me that the Americans had broken through.

We were lined up and marched out of the camp. The guards had changed into civilian clothes despite us advising them to keep their uniforms on or the allies would look on them as spies. They had been told that the Americans would execute them. They were frightened of the Americans but they were even more frightened of the Russians. We couldn't have gone more than two miles when we saw the American tanks coming down the road. The guards took to their heels and ran and we were left standing there in a group and the Yanks went right by. They didn't stop. They were forward troops and couldn't slow down but they shouted and waved and threw cigarettes and chocolates. A jeep pulled up and the officer in it told us to stay where we were. Transport would be coming to pick us up and sure enough, that evening, lorries came for us and took us to a camp. We seemed to be travelling a long way but that didn't bother us, we were getting nearer home all the time. They told us that we would be home the next day and we hung about all the following day waiting for the planes to land. Then we were told that there was thick fog in England and we had to wait until the next day. We didn't have a meal. There were over a thousand of us waiting and they didn't have the supplies but there was plenty of cigarettes and chocolate. I was still wearing my French uniform jacket and a couple of French women hugged and kissed me. They thought I was French.

Then the aeroplanes came in, big American aircraft. I can't describe my feelings. We were going home. It was the first time most of us had flown and I think I was the only one that wasn't sick. We had been given bags when we boarded in case we felt ill but I didn't need mine. I was too occupied looking at the ships and the sea beneath us. Then we saw the English coast and everyone went very quiet and there were a few tears.

We landed at an aerodrome near London and were taken to a hangar where there were long tables and the W.R.V.S. were there with meals for us but we couldn't eat them. I thought we would be able to go straight home but we were transferred to another camp. reissued with new kit and given medicals and then we were allowed home. I went straight to my sweetheart in Colsterworth and we were married a week to the day that I had left Germany in Colsterworth Church. Her grandfather kept pigs and he gave us a ham for our wedding present. My wife was friendly with a couple of American airmen and they gave us tinned fruit. We had a proper wedding even if it was in the middle of the war. Her grandfather worked at the iron ore works and he had a good house and we went and lived with him. There was plenty of room.

I went back to Manchester to visit my family and that was how I discovered that my pay had been stopped as soon as I had been posted missing. It was made up later when they found I was still alive but it had caused my mother a lot of misery.

I was at home for three months and all I had to do was to go and collect my pay from the post office each week. Then we began to think of the future. My wife thought I ought to report back to the authorities so I went down to the office in Wharf Road and I was told to report to Whitworth Street in Manchester for medicals. There were two of us there and we were both listed C2. This meant that we would be discharged and would be entitled to a pension. We then had to report to the officer. He told the other fellow that they didn't have a suitable job for him and he would be demobbed. Then he asked me for my pay book which I gave him and he rubber stamped B2 over the C2 and told me that I could manage light duties and he had a suitable job for me working in the officers' mess. So my wife and I had to face another separation I was demobbed in 1946 and started work straight away working in the R.A.F. shop at Stoke Rochford. Then one day I was asked to pick up a man called Laski from the station. He was buying up the shop where I worked. He said he was sorry he was taking my job away and said he would find me work if I was prepared to move to London but I told him I had a family.

He gave me a £10 tip. That was a lot of money then. I got another job straight away at the ironstone as a painter. When my wife's grandfather died, we had to leave the house straight away but we were lucky. We had one of the new houses in the village. It was such a different world to the one I had left in Manchester. There were comfortable homes and, as long as you were prepared to work, there were jobs and working men like myself were prepared to stand up for ourselves. When I found the trainee was getting more money than I was and I was refused a rise, I left and went to Barfords as a labourer. I became a crane driver and I was there until I retired.

Wedding Day